THE JEWS OF MONTREAL
And Their Judaisms
– *a voyage of discovery*
by MACKAY L. SMITH

MONTREAL 1997

THE JEWS OF MONTREAL

This is not just another dry, quantitative study of the Jewish people of Montreal.
This is the passion of a Montrealer, a *gentile*, for his city and particularly, for the Jews who share it and who have given it so much of its unique character.
MacKay Smith has brought forth a delicious mix of quantitative statistics of the history of the Jews of Montreal, spiced with his own qualitative dressing. The result is a social salad every Montrealer will enjoy.

Every teacher, every student, every member of every ethnic and linguistic group that make up the wonder of Montreal should read this little book, and learn of the origins, the trials, the temptations and the contributions of the Jews of Montreal. In doing so, they will learn that our differences give Montreal its unique appeal.
And that because we're all different,
we are each other.

Copyright © 1997 by MacKay L. Smith

Book design: David Morin
Map design: Richard Bachand
Cover design: Mark Silverstone
Cover photo: MacKay L. Smith

First editor: Jennifer Lokash
Proofreader and Editor: Michael Harris

All rights reserved. No part of this book covered by the copyright herein may be reproduced in any form or by any means—graphic, electronic, or mechanical, including photocopying, recording, taping, of information storage and retrieval systems—without permission in writing from the author, except by a reviewer who may quote brief passages in a review.

Every reasonable effort has been made to trace the ownership of quotes and tables. Information enabling the author to rectify any reference or credit in future printings would be appreciated.

Legal deposits: fourth quarter 1997
National Library of Canada
Bibliothèque nationale du Québec

Canadian Cataloguing in Publication Data

Smith, MacKay L., 1933-
    Jews of Montreal and their Judaisms : a voyage of discovery
Includes bibliographical references and index.
ISBN 0-9683064-0-3
    1. Jews--Quebec (Province)--Montréal--Social conditions. I. Title.
FC2947.9.J4S58 1997   305.89240971428   C97-901264-3
F1054.5.M89J538 1997

Printed and bound in Canada

Published and distributed by:
Aaron Communications
3583 University Street, suite 400
Montreal, Quebec
Canada H3A 2B1
Tel. (514) 281-6526

This book is dedicated to all the Jews still in Quebec.

"A Dry Crust in Peace
Is Preferable to Opulence in Strife"
Eliezer Papo

PREFACE

In a spririted discussion about our childrens' schooling in the multi-culture of Montreal, my long-time friend, Pete Schreter, made one remark that sparked the writing of this book and led me to amass its tottering columns of statistics.

He said he had to 'find a middle ground to accomodate his wife's Sephardic upbringing.' It came to me I didn't understand quite what he was dealing with—nor what being Sephardic really meant.

Thinking about my many Jewish friends I realized I didn't know very much at all about their Judaisms. I felt ignorant and not a little embarassed. So I set out researching what I wanted to know in a variety of domains: sociology and anthropology; the more specific areas of demographic statistics and urban geography and the plethora of problems that lie ahead for the Jewish community. This wealth of opinion and fact I've tried to cobble into data as hard and objective as I could to produce a clearer perspective on this varied and changing community.

Acknowledgements

I've received so much help and encouragement from every one of the interviews, discussions and events I've attended that the list I could write down would be almost endless.

So here are the main actors:
- Neil Caplan of Vanier College—a friend who gave many helpful comments
- Ephraim Massey—poet, mountain climber and friend
- Saul Panofsky—who knows almost everything
- Charles Shahar—a demographic wizard at the Federation of Community Jewish Agencies
- Lonny Weatherby of the McLennan Library at McGill—who seems to know of every book in the stacks
- Claude Yelle of Statistics Canada—who gave me many hints on how to get those statistics
- Morton Weinfeld of McGill University
- Ronald Finegold of the Jewish Public Library
- Steven Drysdale of the Federation of Community Jewish Agencies
- and all those others still in Quebec trying to live in our multi-ethnic society.

Thank you.

TABLE OF CONTENTS

Introduction 11
Part I Historic & Demographic Information
  Chapter 1. Canada 15
  Chapter 2. Quebec 23
  Chapter 3. Montreal 29
Part II Judaisms
  Chapter 4. World 45
  Chapter 5. Judaism 51
  Chapter 6. Mediterranean and European Jews 61
  Chapter 7. Sephardim 65
  Chapter 8. Ashkenazim 69
  Chapter 9. Sephardim in Montreal 85
  Chapter 10. Ashkenazim in Montreal 91
Part III Problems
  Chapter 11. Jewish Women and Equality 97
  Chapter 12. Fertility 103
  Chapter 13. Outmarriage 105
  Chapter 14. Aging and Poverty 111
  Chapter 15. Associations and Organizations 121
  Chapter 16. The Money Web 125
Part IV Biases
  Chapter 17. Anti-Semitism 137
  Chapter 18. The Holocaust 143
  Chapter 19. Dualism 151
  Chapter 20. Nationalism 155

Part V What is to be done?
    Chapter 21. External Rapprochement 161
    Chapter 22. Internal Rapprochement 169
    Chapter 23. Continuity 173
    Chapter 24. Conclusion 181

Appendix
I   Food and religious days 188
II   Synagogues and cemeteries 190
III   Literature and film 192
IV   Lists of groups and associations associated with Montreal and with Israel 195
V   Interviews and discussions 200
VI   Additional demographics 202
VII   Additional bibliography 205
VIII   Glossary 207
Index 210

Tables

Part I
Table 1: Canadian Jews by Religion—1991 16
Table 2: Canada's Jewish population in cities 18
Table 3: Jews in specific areas of Quebec by religion 24
Table 4: Languages of Jews in Quebec 1991 26
Table 5: Population by District–Greater Montreal–Jews by religion . 32
Table 6: Place of Birth by Year of Immigration 36
Table 7: Selected main ethnic groups in Montreal 1991 37

Part II
Table 8: Jewish World Population through the Ages 46
Table 9: Countries with Jewish Population—1993 and late 1930's 46
Table 10: European Countries—1930's and 1993 47
Table 11: Jews in Israel—1988 48
Table 12: U.S.A. Jewish Population 1878-1990 48
Table 13: Simple Differences—Ashkenazim vs. Sephardim 62
Table 14: Jews in the World (1984) 63
Table 15: Jews in Islamic Countries 66
Table 16: Ashkenazi Judaism: differences between West and East 72
Table 17: Some differences of rules and customs between Reform, Conservative and Orthodox Judaisms. 76
Table 18: Montreal's Sephardic Community—1994 86

Table 19: Orthodox Hasidism in Greater Montreal 92
Table 20: Simplified schematic view of Judaism 93
Part III
Table 21: Religious Parallels 94
Table 22: Dominance of Gender—major religions 98
Table 23: Fertility Analysis—AJYB 1981 103
Table 24: Outmarriage Selected Areas (1991) 105
Table 25: Jewish Age Groups in Montreal 111
Table 26: Percentage of Selected Jewish Age Groups in Montreal .. 112
Table 27: Sephardic population by district and age—1986 113
Table 28: Ashkenazi population by district and age—1986 113
Table 29: Evolution in the Percentage of People aged 65 and over, by Ethnic Group, Quebec 1931-1981 115
Table 30: Average Age of Mortality 115
Table 31: Life Expectancy of Selected Areas—Montreal, 1976 116
Table 32: Ages of Three Religious Groups 116
Table 33: Jewish Elderly Population by District 117
Table 34: Poor Jewish Elederly (65+) by distribution—1986 118
Table 35: Fed. C.J.A. Collections 1987, '92-'95 127
Table 36: Revenue Stream of Fed. C.J.A. 127
Table 37: Montreal Foundations—Giving Stream 130
Table 38: Selected Foundations (over 1 million in Assets, 1993) 131
Part V
Table 39: Parallel Clubs 162
Table 40: First Official Language spoken 3,091,115—1991 162
Table 41: Single responses—Language on Montreal Selected areas 163
Table 42: Selected main ethnic groups in Montreal 1991 165
Table 43: Jewish Youth 15-24 (by religion) 176
Table 44: Problems of continuity 177
Table 45: Jewish population in major cities - 1996 202
Table 46: Jewish Population centers in U.S.A. 205

Maps
Map 1: Canada's cities and towns with selected Jewish Communities 19
Map 2: Quebec's cities and towns with selected Jewish Communities 25
Map 3: Population by district-Greater Montreal-Jews by religion 33
Map 4: Sephardic and Ashkenazi populations by district and age ... 114
Map 5: Language in Montreal selected areas 164

Graphics
Graphic 1: American Outlook 107

INTRODUCTION

By definition, every ethnic group has its own characteristics and often is diverse within itself.

When personal stress rises and when these problems attain some significance, every group exhibits some degree of phobism. The level of protection needed for the family, or for the group itself, creates, or recreates, tribalism. Nevertheless, one can question whether it is for the common good to encourage ethnicity or to seek to form a more homogeneous society in the broader context of a country.

As a social creature, almost everyone lives in a particular mileu. In Montreal, Jews are a driving force, and their religion is multi-faceted. This study offers a view on their demographics, on the basis of their thought, and on the difficult and different problems within the community.

> "The insider draws on a special empathy, and inward familiarity the outsider may never attain. The outsider, however, takes less for granted, and may therefore bring to bear a more critical attitude, a move demanding standard of judgment, and a wider range of reference. When a book addresses both insiders and outsiders the writer crosses a mine field of rival sensibilities, and his own particular vulnerabilities become glaringly apparent."[1]

At the beginning of my investigation, the first move I made was to go over to the Bibliophile Book Store and ask for information. I emerged with three books, and hid away in the McLennan Library of McGill University. Later, somewhat confused, I had my first interview with the late Rabbi C. Bender—the voyage had started.

This book is in four parts:

The preliminary section deals mostly with demographic statistics within Canada combined with a number of personal interviews.

The next area covered concerns how Judaism has spread in the world and particularly in Montreal.

Part 3 covers the quandaries that I have found that affect all Jews in Montreal. My biases do show here—I hope fairly.

Part 4 is the end of my voyage of discovery and its conclusions.

I do not pretend to have any earth-shattering opinions, even after 7 years of research as most of the material is available somewhere. Academics will miss the copious footnotes that would have been beneath the text on each page. Readers who enjoy a book without references can skip them. And the appendices will satisfy those who have waded through this book and amazingly want more.

The primary purpose of this study is to help all ethnic communities in Montreal realize their priorities and be able to continue to exist in the cosmopolitan milieu of our wonderful city.

I hope you know a bit more about the Jewish Community when you finish.

MacKay L. Smith, September 1997

References

1. Higham, John. *The Pot that Didn't Melt* (on American Jews) N.Y. Review of Books Apr. 12, 1990, p.11-13.

PART I

HISTORIC AND DEMOGRAPHIC INFORMATION

CHAPTER 1

CANADA

I took my new McGill library card and went to the Documents section and copied all the statistics I could find on the Jews living in Canada from the first census of 1831 to 1986—later to 1991 as the years of this study stretched on. Then I phoned up Statistics Canada, and spoke with Claude Yelle.

I realized that no one had gathered all this information together and explained it—not since Mr. Louis Rosenberg had published his works of demographics in the 1930s to 1950s. I was encouraged that my point of view (blending statistics with opinions and facts about the Jewish community) might suggest a new perspective.

Canada
In 1991, Canada's population was 26,994,045. The Jewish communities totalled 318,070 by religion. Statistics Canada has given totals by ethnicity and by religion in the past, while Mr. J. Torczyner uses a different definition:

> "A Jew is someone who identifies him/herself as being `Jewish by religion', or `Jewish by religion and Jewish by ethnic origin' or `Jewish by ethnic origin with no religion.'"[1]

Thus, the only group excluded are those persons who identify themselves as Jewish ethnically but with a religion other than Jewish. Ethnic Jews, as well as secular Jews with no religious affiliation are all included in this definition. The study of Torczyner et al. gives a total of 356,315 Jews in Canada.

Table 1: Canadian Jews by Religion—1991

Newfoundland	125
P.E.I.	85
Nova Scotia	1,950
N.B.	875
Quebec	97,735
Ontario	175,640
Manitoba	13,670
Sask.	1,375
Alberta	9,945
B.C.	16,565
Yuk.	45
N.W.T.	60
Statistics Canada	318,070

In 1752, the first group of Jews from Europe settled in Halifax. Under the French rule in the 18th century, all non-Catholics were forbidden in French Canada. After the English populated the St. Lawrence, the Jewish population concentrated in Montreal. In 1768, the first synagogue was established—Shearith Israel. In 1803, Jews were allowed to settle in Upper Canada. In 1856, the first synagogue in Toronto was The Sons of Israel. Victoria, in 1863, in the midst of a gold rush, built its synagogue. With the coming of the railhead at Vancouver, the Jewish population in Victoria declined and Vancouver's first synagogue was chartered in 1890. The harsh conditions on the Prairies hindered the building of synagogues in many communities, except in Wappela where a synagogue was built in 1888; with the help of Baron de Hirsch another community, Hirsch, started a synagogue in 1892; both of these were in Saskatchewan.

These small communities of Jews presented no threat to the Protestant and Roman Catholic economic or political structures. However, this was to change when large groups, of many origins from Europe, immigrated to Canada and changed its ethnic makeup after 1900.

All migration has come to Canada in waves, prompted by oppression or by opportunity. J. Kage listed the years between 1905-1916 as the main surge of Jewish immigration to Canada, totalling 123,901, and averaging 8,900/year. Between 1917-30 the average dropped to 4500 and plummeted in 1931-1944 to 730/year.[2]

Before 1900 there was little communication between the scattered Jewish communities in Canada. However, with this 1905-1916 influx of immigration, a great many groups became institutionalized. The nascent Zionist, Socialist and Communist movements commanded sizeable followings. The fragmentation of the communities resulted in imperceptible political or social clout for the growing population of Jews. Jews across Canada, realizing this, established the Canadian Jewish Congress in 1919. Weak as it was at that time, the Congress gave some focus for the Jews of Canada to gather together and feel unified.

Between World War I and World War II, all the established Jewish communities expanded; their people entered into economically sustaining enterprises and became active in their communities. This energy often collided with barriers in education, commerce, recreation.

These barriers even continued during World War II. Wishing to defend the free country of Canada, a total of 16883 (men and women)—10% of Canada's Jewish population—enlisted in, and helped the armed forces. 429 Jews died for Canada, including 104 from Quebec.[3]

After World War II, there was a consolidation of Jewish communities into large urban centers.

The social barriers began to fall. As the Jews became part

of each larger community, schools, hospitals, clubs, associations and business firms finally welcomed them. They now had a sense of "shelter and safety". Their quest for security seemed assured.

Table 2: Canada's Jewish population in cities (Map 1)

	1931	1951	1971	1991
Toronto	46,845	66,870	107,370	151,115
Montreal	57,736	80,788	102,592	96,710
Vancouver	2,407	5,566	10,730	14,300
Winnipeg	17,512*	16,266*	19,380*	13,325
Ottawa/Hull	3,316	4,484	6,645	9,915
Calgary	1,622	2,094	3,710	5,455
Hamilton	2,636	3,158	3,340	4,465
Edmonton	1,057	1,748	2,865	4,040
London	583	871	1,755	2,190
Windsor	2,367	2,330	2,525	1,560
Halifax	5,820	1,012	1,365	1,480
St. C./Niagara	483	735	970	1,150
Victoria	120	115	320	965
Kitchner	415	434	1,115	805
Saskatoon	691	687	585	615
Oshawa	171	298	415	455
Regina	1,010	740	865	485

*Greater Winnipeg area
Statistics Canada — by religion

Notes

1. Torczyner, Jim; Brotman, Shari; Viragh, Kathy. *Demographic Challenges Facing Canadian Jewry: Initial findings from the 1991 Census* Montreal, McGill Consortium for Ethnicity and strategic Social Planning. 1993. p.5
2. Kage, Joseph. *With Faith and Thanksgiving.* Montreal, 1962. FC 5033J3K3, p.259-60
3. Bookman Max. "Canadian Jews in Uniform" *Can. Jewish Reference Book.* 1963 Ottawa 1963, p. 112-124.

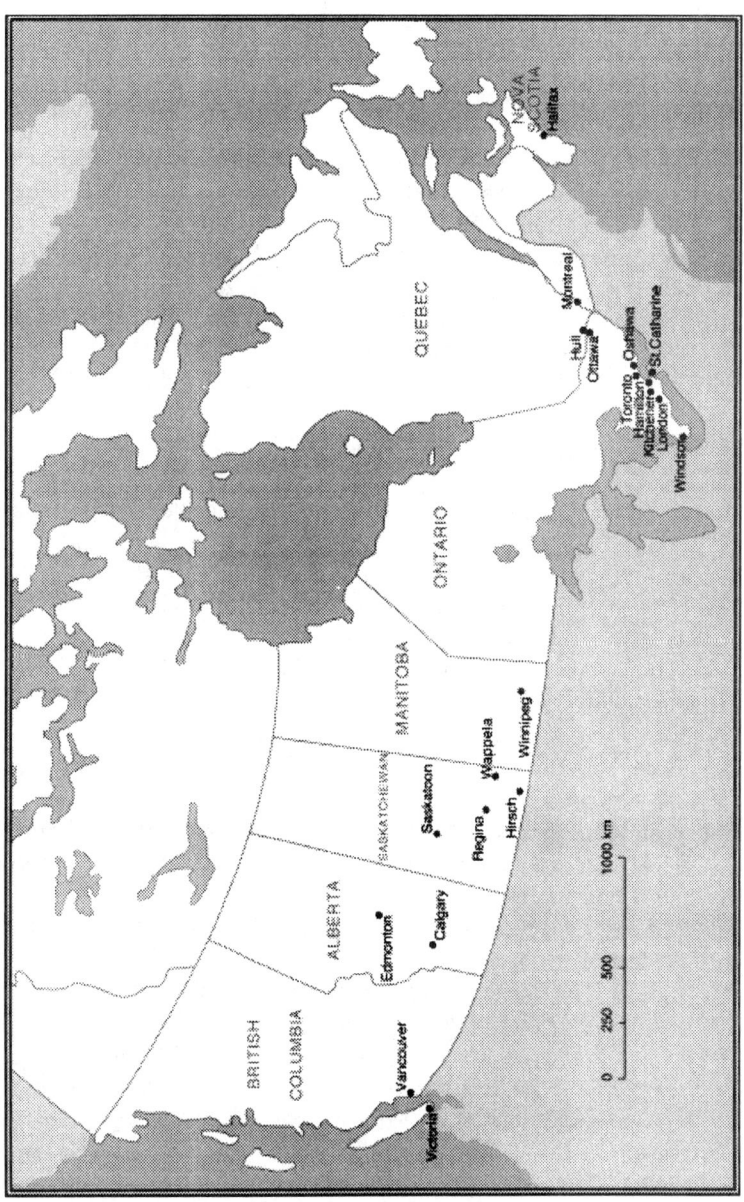

Map 1: Canada's cities with Jewish Communities

References

Canada

Abella, Irving. *A Coat of Many Colours*. Two centuries of Jewish life in Canada. Toronto 1990. FC 106 J5 A23.

Arbin, Paul and Coté Louis-Marie *Bibliography of the History of Quebec and Canada* 4th Ed. Quebec 1990. Inst. Q. de Recherche sur la Culture. Vol. 1 & 2. Z 1382 A83

Aubery, Pierre and Kattan, N. *Juifs et Canadiens*. Montreal 1967 F 5033 J3 J8

Barth, F., *Ethnic Groups and Boundaries: The Social Organization of Cultural Differences*. Boston 1965. GN 320 E77

Beierbach, Levi. "The Jews in Canada - Alberta & the Yukon". *CJN* Apr.6 1995. p.9

Bissoondath, Neil. *Selling Illusion: The Cult of Multiculralism in Canda*. Toronto 1994.

Bookman Max. "Canadian Jews in Uniform" *Can. Jewish Reference Book*. 1963 Ottawa 1963, p. 111-128.

Bronfman Collection of Jewish Canadiana 1962. Z6373C3M6x

Brown, Michael G. *Jewish Foundations in Canada to 1914*. Ph.D. Thesis, St. U. of N.Y. in Buffalo 1976 FC 106 J5 B76

Brym, R.J. *The Jews in Canada* R. Brym, W. Shaffir & M. Weinfeld, editors. Don Mills, 1993.

Brym, Robert J. "The rise and decline of Canadian Jewry? A socio-demographic profile" from *Who's Who in Can. Jewry*—Lipistz, 1989. p. 37-51.

Cohen Steven. *Jewish Identity in Canada: National character, regional diversity and emerging trends*. CRB Foundation, Montreal, 1991, 55 pages. (Survey of 972 households in Canada)

Davids, Leo. "Canadian Jewry: Some recent census findings". *AJYB* 85: 191-201. E184 J5A6

Davids, Leo. 'The Canadian Jewish Pop. Picture: Today and Tomorrow" from *Who's Who in Can. Jewry*. Lipsitz.

Elazar, D., & Waller, H. *Maintaining Consensus* 1990. FC 106 J5E43

Godfrey, Sheldon J. *Search Out the Land, The Jews and the Growth of Equality in British Colonial America 1740-1867*. Montreal 1995.

Gottesman, Dr. Eli *Canadian Jewish Reference Book and Directory 1963*. Ottawa 1963.

Halli, Shiva, Trovato, Frank, & Driedger, Leo. *Ethnic Demography*. Ottawa, 1990.

Kaellis, Eugene. "Jews and Canadian Multiculturalism" *Viewpoints* 21, 1, 1992: 6.

Knight, Bryan. *Voices of Canadian Jews*. Montreal, 1988. FC106 J5K55.

Lipsitz, Edmond Y. (ed.) *Canadian Jewry Today: Who's Who in Canadian Jewry*. FC 106 J5C 428. Downsview 1989.
Love, Myron. "The Jews in Canada - Manitoba/Saskatchewan". *CJN* June 8 1995. p.9
Lucow, Maurice. "The Jews in Canada - British Columbia & N.W.T." *CJN* March 23 1995. p.9.
Paris, Erna *Jews, An Account of their Experiences in Canada* Toronto 1980. FC 106 J5 P37.
Rischin,Moses (ed.) *Jews of North America*. Detroit 1987 E184 J5J67
Rosenberg, Louis. *Canada's Jewish Community*. Canadian Jewish Community Service #1. Canadian Jewish Population Studies. Montreal, 55.
Rosenberg, Louis. *Canada's Jews*.Montreal 1939. Bureau of Soc. & Econ. Research C.J.C., Montreal 1989. (Reissued 1993 with help of Morton Weinfeld.)
Sharp, Rosalie; Abella, Irving; Goodman, Edwin. *Growing Up Jewish, Canadians Tell Their Own Stories*. Toronto 1997.
Torczyner, Jim; Brotman, Shari; Viragh, Kathy. *Demographic Challenges Facing Canadian Jewry: Initial findings from the 1991 Census* Montreal, McGill Consortium for Ethnicity and strategic Social Planning. 1993.
Trovato, Frank and Grindstaff, Carl (editors) *Perspective on Canada's Population*, Toronto, 1994 HB-3529P.47
Trudel, R., Leclerc, Y., et al. *Deux Québec dans un: rapport sur le développement social et démographique* Gov't of Quebec—conseil des Affairs sociales. Boucherville 1989. H83530 Q4 D48.
Tulchinsky, Gerald. "Recent development in Can. Jew. Histography" *Can Ethnic Studies* 14, 2 (1982) 11-125.
Tulchinsky, Gerald. *Taking Root the origins of the Canadian Jewish Community* (to 1920) Toronto, 1992. FC 106 J5 T86.
Vigod, Benard L. *The Jews in Canada*, 1984 Booklet #7 Canadian Ethnic Groups FC 106J5V54.
Weinfeld, Martin. "Canadian cultural pluralism & its implication for the Jewish Community". *Shofar* 5, 2 (1987) 1-7.
Weinfeld M., Shaffir W., & Cotler I. (editions). *The Canadian Jewish Mosaic* Toronto 1981. FC 106 J5C28.
Zeilig, Martin. "Jewish Identity in Canada". *Outlook* Jan-Feb 1992. p11-12.
National Archives Newsletter *Can Jewish Congress*
National Archives of Canada. Manuscript division. Canadian Jewish Archives Program.

Canada Immigration
Abella, I & Troper, H. *None is Too Many*. 3rd edition. Toronto, 1991.

Arnold, Janice. "Quebec's changing face". *C.J.N.* June 17 & 24, 1993, p. 1 and 2.
Belkin, Simon I. Through Narrow Gates: A Review of Jewish Immigration 1840-1940, C.J.C. publication, Montreal, 1966
Burnet, Jean R. & Palmer, Howard. *"Coming Canadian"* Toronto, 1989. FC104 B87
Driedger, Leo (ed.) *Ethnic Canada* Toronto, 1987.
Grunau, Esther.*Ethiopian Jews in Canada: a process of constructing an identity*. Mtl 1995, M.A. Theses McGill University A542M31996G786
Kage, Joseph. *With Faith and Thanksgiving*. Montreal, 1962. FC 5033J3K3
Kalbach,W.E. "Growth & distribution of Canada's ethnic population" in *Canadian Ethnic Mosaic*. Toronto, 1978. FC 104C35
Kalbach W.E. & McVey A. *The Demographic Basis of Canadian Soc.* (2nd ed.) Toronto, 1979. HB3529K34.
Lachapelle, Regen & Henripin, J. *Demolinguistic situation in Canada*. HB3529L3313
Lambert R.D. & J. E. Curtis. *Social Stratification: Canada* (2nd ed.) Toronto, 1979 HN11029S62.
Luciuk, L.Y., & Kordan, B.S. *Creating a Landscape: A Geography of Ukrainians in Canada* # Folio G1116E1L83, Toronto, 1989.
Millett, David. "A typology of religion origin suggested by Can. census" *Sociological Analysis* 30: 108-119.
Overbeck, J. *Population & Canadian Society*. HB 3529,093 Toronto, 1980, pages 140-151.
Poirier, Marie. Writing on 1890-1914 Immigration "Everyone in Europe and England wanted to send the poor Jewry away".
Sarna, J.D. "Jewish Immigration to North America: The Canadian Experience (1870-1900)" *Jewish Journal of Sociology* #18, 1976: 31-41.
Shaffir, William. "Jewish Immigration to Canada" in *Two Nations, Many Cultures* ed. J.L. Elliot Scarborough, 1979.
Simmons, James. "Recent trends & patterns in Canadian settlement 1976-81" *Centre for Urban and Comm. Study*, U. of T.: Report #23, July 1984, Toronto. HT127-S546 1984.
Simmons, James and Simmons, Robert. *Urban Canada* (2nd ed.) Toronto, 1974. HT127 555X
Tzuk, Yogen. *History of the Jews in Canada: a Textbook for high school students*. Toronto, 1992.

CHAPTER 2

QUEBEC

My family had a cottage near Ste-Agathe during the 1940s and 1950s when Ste-Agathe was a centre for many Jews during the summer. Nearby were the summer camps—B'nai Brith, Unzer, Massad, Kvutza, Pripstein's, Kinderveldt and Hiawatha. Quite a few cars sported American licence plates, and the town was crowded with tourists coming out of the Jewish hotels such as Hotel Vermont, Rabiner's, Castle des Monts, Manoir Ste-Agathe, Kaiserman's and the Laurentian Hotel. Many of the hotels had Kosher dining rooms.

I was reminded of this summer scene by Jerry Peters as we talked when I went to buy a paper at his Avenue Smoke Shop. He is a cantor, and he sang in these hotels in his late teens and early twenties. Musicians and storytellers such as Nat Raider, Jackie Kahanne and Lenny Rubin entertained at these hotels. Ste-Agathe for Jerry was a new life, because in his earlier years his family couldn't afford to get to Ste-Agathe and "went to the country" by going to Plage Laval.

Quebec

Most Jewish immigrants to Quebec gathered in ports of the St. Lawrence—Quebec City, Trois-Rivières and Montreal. Itinerant travellers fanned out through Quebec to ply their trades, but, as communications improved after World War II, most Jews moved to Montreal. This left Jewish families in many of the outlying communities without regular religious services. For instance, Quebec City's Beth Israel congregation, founded in 1852, sold its synagogue in 1990, as its membership had dropped from 100 families in the 1950s and 1960s, to 25 in 1990. A new smaller synagogue has been bought, the congregation's cemetery has been declared a National Historical Site, and the community still has approximately 25 families. Synagogues in Sherbrooke, Trois Rivières, and St. Jean have recently closed.[1]

A community of Jews in Boisbriand, the Hasidic (Tash) sect, have left Montreal for a life of a more isolated nature. In Ste-Agathe, the House of Israel synagogue has a membership of 700 in the summer months. Sainte-Sophie has had a Jewish community for 100 years and is beside the Rivière Jourdain.

Table 3: *Jews in specific areas of Quebec (Map 2)*

	1921	'31	'41	'51	'61	'71	'81	'91
Rimouski to Gaspé	62	40	54	21	27	35	15	10
Lac St. Jean	24	37	45	23	24	30	30	25
Quebec City	427	471	423	442	495	395	230	155
Trois-Rivières	175	116	143	104	104	40	30	15
Sherbrooke	373	267	378	328	313	250	205	140
St. Jean-Iberville	86	102	110	108	61	45	25	10
Laurentians (Ste-Sophie, Ste-Agathe)	456	419	383	371	332	300	211	160
Hull	122	58	30	25	58	85	105	120
Hudson-Vaudreuil	0	13	20	25	25	70	105	135
North-West (Rouyn etc.)	0	62	203	176	102	70	45	37
Broisbriand	0	0	0	0	80	120	440	875

25

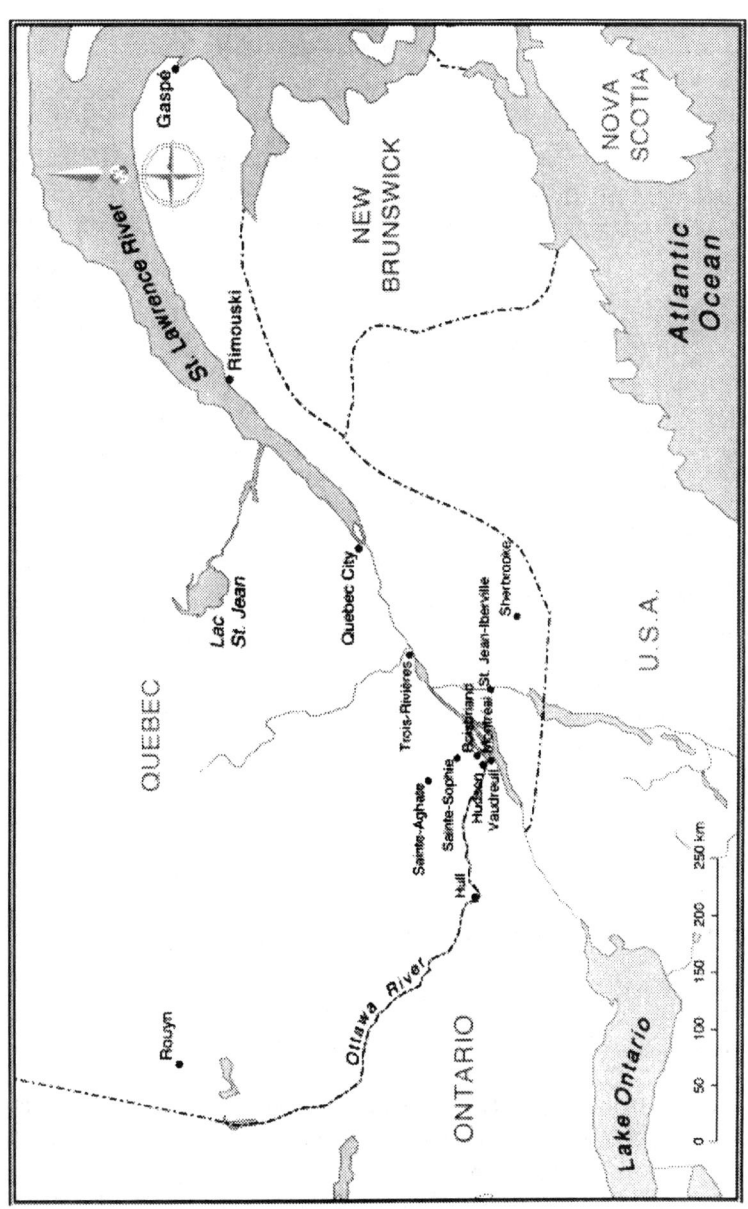

Map 2: Jews in specific areas of Quebec

Interestingly, the spectrum of languages of the Jews of Quebec is varied.

Table 4: Languages of Jews in Quebec 1991 (single response) Jews in Quebec by religion 97,730. Total responses to Language 94,880

English	54,780
French	14,100 *
Yiddish	9,205
Polish	1,590
German	1,240
Spanish	1,230 *
Arabic	1,070 *
Italian	250
Portuguese	135 *
Dutch	80
Greek	30 *
Ukrainian	10
Others	11,015 **
Multiple response	1,845 *

Statistics Canada
* probably Sephardic
**probably many are Russian

Notes

1. *Canadian Jewish News.* Quebec City. p. 7

References

Anctil, Pierre. Juifs et réalités juives du Québec. Québec, 1984. FC 290 J5 J93.

Brown, Michael. *Jew or Juif: Jews French Canadian and Anglo-Canadians 1759-1914.* Phila. 1986. Founded on his Ph.D. Thesis U. of N.Y. Buffalo 1976. FC J5 B76 1976.

Bouchard, Gérard. *Cahiers Québécois de Démographie* See vol. 18 #2 p. 286 & 317; vol. 19 #1 Gérard Bouchard. "Représentation de la population de la société québécoise: L' apprentissage de la diversité" p. 7-28.

Bruneau, Pierre. *Les Villes moyennes au Québec* Sillery 1989. HT 127 B79.

Caldwell, Gary & Eric Waddell *English of Quebec: Majority to Minority Status.* Quebec 1982. (Inst. Q de Recherche SW Catholic) FC 2950.5 C35.

Caldwell Gay *Anglophone Quebec of Montreal Area in the Seventies.* Quebec: 1980. HS 3530 Q4C 337.

Choinière, Robert "Integration géographique et sociale de la population Juive à la société Québécoise". *Cahiers Québécois de démographie* vol. 10 #3 déc. 1982, p. 381-396.

Choinière, Robert & Robitaille, Norbert. "The aging of ethnic groups in Quebec" in *Ethnic Demography* p. 253-271. ed. S. S. Halli. Ottawa 1990 HB 3529E4.

Cohen, Stanley. "An interview with Saul Hayes" *Viewpoints* 9 #4, 1976: 5-25 (especially p. 5)

Farnsworth, Clyde. "A Vanishing Community." Montreal *Gazette* Aug. 22, 1995, p. A4.

Henripin, Jacques. *Naître ou ne pas être* HQ 766 5C ZH46. Quebec 1989.

———. *La fin de la revanche des berceaux: qu'en pensent les Québécoises?* Montreal, 1974. HQ766.5C2H45x

Henripin, Jacques & Peron, Yves. "The demogrpahic Transition of the Province of Quebec" p. 373-391 in W.P. Ward. *The Social Development of Canada—Readings.* Richmond 1983.

Henripin, Jacques & Martin Y. *La population du Québec et de ses régions 1961-1981.* Quebec 1964. HB3530Q4H4.

———. *La Population du Québec: d'hier à demain.* Montreal, 1981. HB 3530 Q4P67

Joy Richard. *Languages in Conflict* 1972 and new edition 1991. FC 145 B55 J68, JL 25 J6 1972

Kantrowitz, Jack. "Jews in the New Quebec" *Viewpoints.* 10, 1 (Spring 1979) 5-10. AD 91-V54 x.

Laforest, Guy. Review of "Nationals & the Politics of Culture in Quebec" by R. Handler. *C.J. of Pol. Sc.* 21 Dec. 88, p. 842-843.

L'anglais, Jacques. *Québec de demain et les communautés culturelles* Montreal, 1990. FL 2950 A1 Q43.

L'anglais, Jacques, Rome David. *Juifs et Québécois Français 200 ans d'histoire commune,* 1986. FC 1950 J5 L35.

LaRoque, Hertel. *L'admissable juif, maître chez-nous.* Montreal, 1964. F 5033 J3L3

Lubin, Martin. "The Politics of Social Policy in Quebec: The Case of Bill 65 (1971) and the Jewish community." *Quebec Studies* 11 (Spring 1983): 43-70. (Services du Sante).

McRoberts, Kenneth. *Quebec: Social Change & Political Crisis* (3rd ed.) Toronto, 1988. JL 242 M25X

Pirie, Margaret C. *Patterns of Mobility and Assimilation: A Study of the Toronto Jewish Community.* New Haven, 1957, Ph.D. Thesis.

Richler, Mordecai. *This Year in Jerusalem.* Toronto, 1994.

Rome, David. "Reflections in the History of Jews in Quebec" From *Who is a Québécois*. Vachon & L'Anglais 1983. FC 2950 A1-Q513.
Rome, David. "Jews in Anglophone Quebec" from *The English of Quebec: From majority to minority status*" Quebec 1982. (Inst. Québécois de Recherche) p. 159-176. FC 2950.5 c35.
Senecel, Andre & Crane, Namey. *Quebec Studies*—A selected bibliography Burlington, V.T. 1982. by Information Center on Canada (P.O. Box 627) 05402. Z1392 Q354
Teboul Victor. *Mythe & Images du Juif au Québec* Montreal 1977. FC 2950 J5 T4.
Vachon, F. & L'Anglais, J. (Ed.) *Who is a Quebecois* Montreal 1983. FC 2950 A1 Q 513.
Vauqeois, Denis. *Les Juifs et la Nouvelle France*. F 5033 J3V3. Trois-Rivières,1968.
Waller, H. & Weinfeld, M. "The Jews of Quebec and "La fait français"" from *Can. Jewish Mosaic* p. 415-439.
Weinfeld, Morton. *Ethnic sub-economy: explication & analysis of a case study of the Jews of Montreal*. Montreal, 1980. FC 2947.9 J4W4.
Weinfeld, Morton. "Quebec contemporary Jewish milieu" Inst. Québécois de Recherche sur la culture. Montreal 1984.
    Also see "The Jewish Quebec: An overview" in *Community & the Individual Jew* (1986): 85-109.
Bibliographie sélective sur les communautés culturelles à Montréal. Montreal 1984. Z 1392 Q38535.
Gov. Que. *Deux Québec dans un* Conseil des affaires sociales Boucherville 1989. HB3530 Q4 D48.
Gazette Dec. 22, 90, p. 16.
    "Stopping Montrealers' exodus" Oct. 3, 1994.
    "Exodus of Montreal Jews slows" Aug. 24, 1994, p. 1 &13.
Canadian Jewish News. Quebec City
    Oct. 15, 92 p. 7. "Quebec City has new shul"
    Aug. 8: 94, p. 5. "230-year-old Quebec cemetery named national historical site."
Canadian Jewish News. Ste Agathe
    July 30, 1992 "Little house of Israel boasts big numbers" p. 16.
    Dec. 22 1990 "Ski-and-party approach boosts fortunes of laurentian shul" p. 16.

CHAPTER 3

MONTREAL

I guess the first Jewish people I knew were fellow classmates at St. George's School. I went back there recently and found the names of friends who had been there—some had moved away, some tragically had passed away. Fortunately, I was able to interview Dr. Herta Guttman, and we had a joyous reunion 50 years after we'd first met.

My first business experience with a Jew was at an early age. I "subcontracted" the delivery of The Gazette and the Montreal Star from a small bent man named "Issy" who gave me the newspapers at Cote-des-Neiges and Trafalgar. I did the Westmount mountain route of 27 papers, morning and afternoon. I also worked part-time making deliveries after school for a Jewish couple who ran the candy store inside the Trafalgar Apts. They read newspapers written in what looked to me like Egyptian hieroglyphics, but they told me it was the Yiddish script.

I played hockey on the Bronfman rink, crashed Charles Bronfman's bar mitzvah to eat the sweets, was shot at by Edgar Bronfman with his B-B gun (all hell broke loose between my Dad and his father, Sam), roomed with Howie Ryshpan at boarding school, sat beside a raft of Jews including Jerry Miller and Morty Taffert in Drafting Class at McGill, gravitated to the McGill Union where I tried to beat Jimmy Miller at pool (always unsuccessfully), and kibitzed at the 3¢ game of Hearts, occasionally being allowed to play with the "Immortals".

I got to know Peter Schreter when we roomed together at Survey School at St. Gabriel de Brandon. On returning to Montreal, I was invited to Peter's home. At dinner, for the first time, I ate gefilte fish and had the very sweet red Manichevitz wine. Thinking about it 44 years later, it was the last time for the Manichevitz!

In my youth, I knew many Jews without feeling a bit of the anti-semitism that was rampant at the time. Looking back, I understand that it must have been the progressive schooling at St. Georges' that so stressed equality that prejudice there was a non-issue.

Montreal

In the 19th century, the Jewish population lived in the downtown area of south central Montreal. In 1900, there were only 7000 Jews, most of whom had integrated into the general social fabric of Montreal. The influx of Eastern European Jews increased after 1900, and by 1931, there were 58,000. As the community became more affluent, there was a move to the suburbs that accelerated until 1976. The Parti Québécois victory of that year effectively stopped the growth of the Jewish population of Montreal (see Table #5).

In 1971, Polese et al. demonstrated that the Jewish community was the most concentrated of any ethnic group, especially segregating themselves from the Francophone population: "On pourrait presque parler d'un ville dans la ville, possédant sa propre infrastructure institutionelle." When their economic status increases, there is more "cohabitation en général avec des populations anglophone."[1] Then the Sephardic Morrocan French-speakers arrived and integrated into both the Jewish and French milieus.

The Parti Québécois, scared of their loss of population percentage base[2] and the past weak economic performance of the rurally-bound and agriculturally-oriented French

Quebecers, upgraded their policies on immigrants to bring in French speakers and instituted the Government to become a major player in the intervention of economic policies. According to Anctil, "by controlling public policies in the jurisdictions deemed of provincial significance, such as education, culture, language and public investment, francophones hoped to create a viable political base ... as an alternative to the otherwise solid control of the private capitalist sector by Anglo-Protestants."[3] The P.Q.'s continuous changes in education, involved revisionist teachings via prescribed textbooks and increased hours of French in the classroom, and in language legislation, such as the arguments over Bill 22, Bill 101, and Bill 178, traumatized the Jewish community. They had had no involvement with the Parti Québécois comparable to what they had always had with the provincial Liberal Party (even after this Liberal Party itself had become nationalistic). Because of these Bills and the nationalistic leaning of the Parti Quebecois and even the Quebec Liberal Party, Anglophones began the steady exodus from Quebec which continues to this day.

A study done on Outremont by François Ricour, published in 1964, sets the standards and the ideas for the different sections of Greater Montreal for this study. Splitting up Outremont into five districts—one industrial area, two commercial areas, the parks, and the mountain area—Ricour showed the relief, population density, and Jewish population distribution with conclusions for each district. This paper's statistics were drawn from the 1960 evaluation roll when the Outremont population was 40% French, 34% Jewish, and 26% Italian, Greek, and others. In the 1951 census, the Jewish population peaked at 11,566 with the first decline evident at 9003 in 1961, to the low point of 2845 in 1991.[4]

Table 5: Population by District-Greater Montreal-Jews by religion (Map 3)

Island of Montreal	1931	1941	1951	1961	1971	1981	1991
Old Jewish Quart.	20480	15582	11973	1985	705	335	300
Downtown-West	218	644	705	795	2010	2440	2740
Laurier	8187	10185	6685	*	*	*	*
Mile-End	10590	13120	10026	5025	1010	835	830
Park Extension	3127	3802	2493	3073	915	445	150
Outremont	6760	10306	11566	9003	3955	2765	2845
C.D.N./Wilderton	316	3572	4241	12067	7165	2520	855
Town of Mount-Royal	1	12	298	2617	4305	3720	4010
St-Laurent	9	4	99	7696	10085	8780	8790
Cartierville	7	38	104	692	1520	535	305
Dollard des Ormeaux	0	0	0	16	2150	5775	9150
Westmount	1764	1578	1675	2322	2855	3735	4405
Snowdon	3281	4726	15435	27650	24260	17545	12855
Hampstead	0	52	538	1560	4805	5590	5490
Cote-St-Luc	0	13	34	8307	17460	20495	21160
Notre Dame de Grace	**	**	3521	8214	5665	4625	4540
Montreal West	15	18	25	585	805	990	1040
Verdun	336	442	465	396	360	180	220
Lachine	264	153	69	50	45	40	75
Dorval	19	15	3	252	155	140	160
Pte-Claire	12	1	3	109	115	250	260
Beaconsfield/Bdv.	0	1	18	111	305	415	460
Kirkland/Pierrefonds	0	0	0	20	270	670	820
TOTAL	55306	64264	69976	92545	90920	82795	81460

* included in Old Jewish Quarter, ** included in Snowdon

Off Island	1931	1941	1951	1961	1971	1981	1991
Laval - Chomedey	1	87	3	3403	11005	9085	5335
Boisbriand	0	0	0	80	440	627	875
South Shore	40	48	37	153	227	417	635
TOTAL	41	137	340	3558	11672	10129	6845

Statistics Canada

33

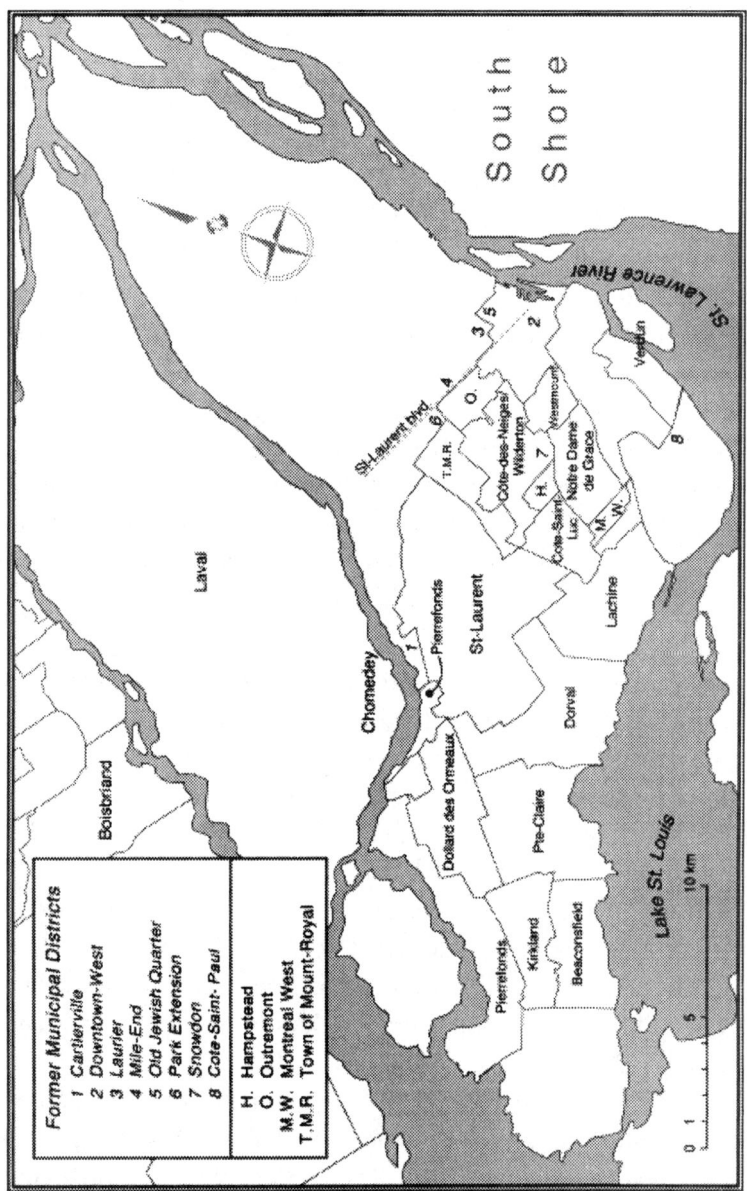

Map 3: *Population by district-Greater Montreal-Jews by religion*

It should be said that growth was impeded in some areas by the conservativism of the ruling English elite that mostly lived in Westmount and upper downtown. Founding groups who started up Hampstead and Town of Mont-Royal put in the houses' deeds of sale that the property was not to be sold to Jews. It wasn't until after World War II, when the leaders of the French and English populations realized the Jews had contributed to the winning of World War II and had an emerging economic clout, that the Jews really came into the mainstream of Montreal life.

The districts that the Jews live in are quite as distinct as Table #5 shows. In 1991, on the Island of Montreal east of St-Laurent Blvd., of a total of 660,000 people, 502,000 are French, 114,00 are Italian, and 730 are Jews, of which 175 live close to St-Laurent Blvd. and 170 live in St-Leonard.[5]

•••

In November of 1991, I interviewed Lou Miller, who was recovering from a heart attack after a distinguished career as a newspaperman for 45 years. During the interview, his wife, Celia, reminded us of their first meeting when Lou's brother had lined up a blind date. They have been "going steady" ever since.

In the 1930s, it took Lou an hour by streetcar and 2 tickets to get home from the Montreal Terminus building—it went to the end of the line at 55th Avenue. Lou got off at 6th Avenue and walked to St. Louis when his family had a general store (now a T.V. store).

At this time, there was a strong Jewish presence in Lachine between 6th and 12th Avenue—the baker Copoloff on 7th Ave., the shoemaker Ferkoff on 8th Ave., the milkman Beramoff, the grocery store of the Kaufman family, and the Kosher meat store of Lazar on 9th.

Most of Lou's early friends were French, from 4th to 6th Aves. Later going to English day school on 16th Ave., he had to run the gauntlet of the French kids who were at the Monastery Ste-Annes on 16th Ave. Many times he would take the shortcut through the graveyard behind the school so he wouldn't get in to a fight. The synagogue Beth Israel was on 9th Ave. between St. Louis and Notre Dame and was known as the Rich One's Synagogue. The poorer Jews had a shul north of the CPR tracks; this synagogue closed in the 1930s. Beth Israel closed in 1944 when the Jewish population moved to Snowdon and the newly developing Cote-St-Luc.

The area around 9th, Notre Dame and Victoria was the hub of the Lachine Jewish Community. There were two theatres—the Empress and Royal Alexander—and most of the Jewish commercial and retail outlets.

The Schecter family still runs a furniture store on St. Louis and the Singer brothers run a sportswear manufacturing company on 6th Ave. Meyer Schecter and the Singers were born above these establishments but now live elsewhere. In the past, industrial concerns were owned by the Swalski, Polichuk and Gameroff families around 6th and 7th Ave.

Lou remembers that the Canadian Army had a post at 6th Ave. during World War II to guard the Lachine Canal. Then Lou moved away from Lachine ending his family's connection that started when his great uncle, who, having one of the contracts to dig out the Lachine Canal, persuaded Lou's grandfather to leave Europe and open up a store for the workmen from Montreal and the Indians from the Reserves who had paddled across the river to work.

Someone should buy the Beth Israel and combine it with the Canada Parks' Lachine exhibits to show the important forgotten historical presence of the Lachine Jews.

Montreal's changing geographic demographics were fuelled by the influx of immigrants from all over the world. The analysis of Torczyner et al. is very enlightening—Table #6 shows their statistics from 1935.

Table 6: Place of Birth, by Year of Immigration to Canada

	<'39	40-49	50-59	<'61	60-69	70-79	80+	Total
Austria	70	105	115	290	10	20	15	335
Belgium		25	90	145		30	55	230
France		25	145	215	200	335	550	1300
Netherlands	40		15	15				15
Germany		165	150	355	45	25	10	435
Italy			60	60	30	10		100
Rest				1445	350	305	235	2335
West Europe	110	320	575	2525	635	725	865	4750
Yugoslavia			20	20				20
Czechoslov	15	165	265	430	45		15	490
Hungary	1425	90	915	1020	350	40	65	1475
Poland	190	1350	1700	4475	295	110	45	4925
Romania		160	765	1115	565	495	140	2315
Rest				1210	140	200	265	1815
East Europe	1630	1765	3665	8270	1395	845	530	11040
USSR				1855	100	505	500	2960
USA				1005	475	690	665	2835
Iraq				200	220	95		515
Morocco, Tunis, Algeria				275	2900	2980	1840	7995
French Middle-East				210	140	360	175	885
Israel				545	365	980	1540	3430
Africa				225	410	160	100	895
Asia				65	20	40	45	170
Japan						20		20
South America				20	75	100	70	265
Spain, Portugal					30	35		85
Other						15	25	40

Torczyner et al. p. 51

To highlight Montreal's cosmopolitan makeup, table #7 shows the main ethnic groups and language spoken in Greater Montreal.

Table 7: Selected main ethnic groups in Montreal 1991—Also by 1st language at home. Greater Montreal 3,091,115.

	Ethnic	Language	
French	1,824,305	2,080,980	
British	166,815	440,870	-English
Italian	165,735	129,615	
Jewish	76,780		-Yiddish 11,255
			-Hebrew 3515
Greek	48,575	45,150	
African	38,650		-mixed
Chinese	34,355	29,020	
Portuguese	32,350	29,780	
Lebanese	28,490		-mixed
Latin Am.	24,905		-with Spanish
Haitian	20,145	24,505	-Creoles
Polish	20,025	17,075	
German	18,935	14,770	
Spanish	18,540	46,570	
Vietnamese	17,790	15,900	
East Indian	16,765		-6 languages
Armenian	13,675	13,825	
Ukrainian	9,940	5,920	
Philippine	9,735	5,370	
Cambodia	6,700	5,250	

Statistics Canada

More Russian Jews have arrived in Montreal since this 1991 census was taken. In 1996, during an interview, Steven Drysdale gave me a figure of 5,000 for the total of Russian Jews in Montreal. After 70 years of not being allowed to practise Judaism, they often have only cultural traditions left. In Russia, the JIAS and the Jewish Agency try to prepare the Russians for emigration by teaching English or French to those going to Canada and Hebrew to those travelling to Israel.

Those immigrants going to Quebec must be ready to learn French, and 100 families are allowed into Quebec per year by the Quebec Government. Those going to the rest of Canada go through regular Canadian channels which are free of language restrictions.

Notes

1. Polése, Marie, Homel Charles, & Bailly Antoine. "La géographie résidentielle des immigrants et des groupes ethniques: Montréal 1971" *INRS—urbanization* (3465 Durhcher Montreal H2X-2C6) Etudes #12. 1978. p.37-8.
2. Joy and Henripin—see page 27
3. Anctil, Pierre. *Le rendez-vous manqué: Les juifs de Montréal face au Québec de l'entre-deux-guerres.* Quebec 1988. FC 2947.9 J4 A52. p.8.
4. Ricour, Françoise "Les Quartiers d'Outremont" *Review de Géographie de Montréal* 18 #1 1964: 65-85. p.76.
5. Statistics Canada 1991. Analysis by author.

References

Abella, Irving. "Dissent and Pluralism in the Montreal Jewish Community: A Historical Survey." *Viewpoints* Vol. XVI, #2, 1988, p. 1-3.

Anctil, Pierre *Forging a viable partnership: the Montreal Jewish community vis à vis the Quebec State.* Feb. 21, 1991. 29 pages.

Anctil, Pierre. *Le rendez-vous manqué: Les juifs de Montréal face au Québec de l'entre-deux-guerres.* Quebec 1988. FC 2947.9 J4 A52.

Anctil, Pierre. "Double majorité et multiplicité ethnoculturelle à Montréal" *Recherches sociographiques* 25, 1984: 441-456.

Bélanger, Marcel. "Le complexe prei: metropolitan Montréalais: une adopte de l'évolution des populations totales" *Rev. Geog. Montreal* 26 (1972): 241-49.

Blanc, Bernadette 1986. "... immigrants à Montréal" *Can. Ethnic St.* 18: 89-108 1986.

Choinière, Robert. "Intégration géographique et sociale de la population Juive à la société Québécoise", *Cahier Québécois de demographie* 10, 3 dec. 1982: 381-396.

Cooper J.L. "The soc. structure of Montreal in the 1850s" *Rapport de la Soc. Hist. Du Canada.* 6-8 Jan. 1956, p. 63.

Elazar, Daniel & Waller Harold. *Maintaining Consensus: The Canadian Jewish Polity in the Postwar World*. Jerusalem 1989. FC 106 J5E43 (1981 Statistics)

Elbaz M. "Ségrégation spatiale et identité ethnique: Les juifs à Montréal." Rapport de recherche, Dept. d'Antro., U. of Laval, 1989.

Fauteux, Martial "La Croissance de la population dans la region de Montréal 1971-81" *C. de Geo. de Québec* 27, 71 (Sept. 83); 165-183.

Gubbay, Aline "Getting to know Jewish Montreal". *A Street Called the Main* Montreal 1989. B-L. FC2947.67 M3 G83.

Jenkins, Kathleen. *Montreal: Island City of the St. Lawrence* Garden City N.Y. 1966. p. 510-516.

Kage, Joseph "The North American Jewish Immigration in Montreal" *Studies and documents immigration and integration in Canada* #11 (Jun 68) FC 1045933, 1-14. Also see FC 106 J5 S933

King, Joe. *Three Score & Ten* Montreal 1987. (J.C.S., 70 years of history.)

Lacoste, Norbert. *Les caractéristiques sociales de la population du Grand Montréal*. Montreal 1950. HC 118 M6L3

Langlois, Andre. "... segregation residentielle à Montréal 1931-71" *Can Geog*, 29, 1985: 197-206.

Mann, Harvey. "The Jews of St. Denis: An Introduction" 8, 2 (fall 1984): 85-89 *Can Jewish Hist. Soc. Journal* (Samuel Jacobs)

Mathews, Georges "l'impact de l'immigration sur le marché du logement dans la région métropolitaine de Montréal de 1961-81". *Gov. of Que.*, Minister of Immigration Int. Nat. de la recherche Scientifique Etudes et documents #6.

Ng, Mun Sing *Some changes in population distribution in Metro Montreal 1951-1981*. Montreal 1987. B-L AS42M37 1987 N436.

Oiwa, Keinosuki *Tradition and social change: An ideological analysis of Montreal Jewish Immigrant ghetto in early 20th century* J.C. Congress, Thesis. FC 2947.9J4038

Polése, Marie, Homel Charles, & Bailly Antoine. "La géographie résidentielle des immigrants et des groupes ethniques: Montréal 1971" *INRS—urbanization* (3465 Durhcher Montreal H2X-2C6) Etudes #12. 1978. 38 pages.

Ramirez, Bruno "Montreal's Italians, the Socioeconomy of Settlement". *Urban History Review* X #1 (Jan. 81) p. 39-48.

Ricour, Françoise "Les Quartiers d'Outremont" *Review de Géographie de Montréal* 18 #1 1964: 65-85.

Robinson, Ira. and Butovsky, Mervin (editors) *Renewing Our Days*. Montreal 1996.

Roiter, Howard. *Here comes Hymie! A novel of Montreal immigrant life* Edmonton, 1990. PS8585 07285 H4.

Rome, David & L'Anglais, Jacques. *The Stones that Speak* Sillery, 1992.
Rosenberg, Louis. "Changes in the geog. distribution of the population of Metro. Montreal 1901-1961". Montreal, Can. Jewish Congress. Bureau of Social and Econ. Res. Dec. 1, 1966, 7 pages.Research paper Sec. A #7 (Stencilled).
Rosenberg, Louis. *The Jewish Population of Montreal.* J.C. Series #4, C.J.C. 1955.
Rosenberg, Louis. *Population characteristics of the Jewish community of Montreal.* J.C. Sries #6, C.J.C.
Roth, Cecil. "The Origin of Ghetto" p. 226-236. From *Personalities & Events in Jewish History*, Philadelphia, 1953. DS 119 R78
Rudin,Ronald. *Forgotten Quebecers: A History of English Quebec 1759-1980.* Quebec 1985. p. 237-41. Jewish Education.
Seidel, J. *The development and social adjustment of the Jewish Community in Montreal.* McGill Thesis 1939. AS42M3 1939 S45.
Shahar, C. *Montreal Jewish Community: Attitudes, Beliefs & Behaviors.* A.J.C.S. Montreal 1991. Survey of a small sample (353) of Jews in Montreal.
Shahar, C. *1986 Census Survey*, A.J.C.S. July 89, Montreal.
Torczyner, James L. *Diversity and continuity: The demographic challenges facing Montreal Jewry.* Montreal: McGill Consortium for Ethnicity & Strategic Social Planning in conjunction with: Council of Jewish Federations—Canada, Federation CJA, Statistics Canada 1994. FC2947.9 J4T67 1994
Tulchinsky. Gerald. "The third solitude: A.M. Klein's Jewish Montreal 1910-1950" p. 96-111. *J. of Can. St.* 19 #2 1984: 96-112.
Tzuk, Yogev. *Jewish communal leadership in Montreal.* Montreal 1984. FC106 J5 T882, 198. Also *Juifs et realitiés juives au Québec* 2950 J5 J93 1984.
Veltman, Calvin. "L'évolution de la ségrégation linguistique à Montréal 1961-81" *Recherches Socio-géographies* 24, 3 (Sept. Dec. 1983) (Movement de population)
Waller, Harold M. & Schreter, Sheldon. *The Governance of the Jewish Community of Montreal.* Study Report #5. Jerusalem 1974. Center for Jewish community Studies FC 2947.9 J4W3.
Waller, Harold. "Montreal weathers the Quebec crisis" From *Maintaining Consensus Part Two* p. 69-150.
Weinfeld, Morton & Eaton, William. *A survey of the Jewish community of Montreal 1979* (Jew. Com. Research Inst. of Montreal). FC 2947.9J459.
Weinfeld, Morton. *The ethnic sub-economy: explication and analysis of a case study of Jews in Montreal.* McGill U., 1980. FC 2947.9 S4 W4
Weintraub, William. *City Unique: Montreal Days and Nights in the 1940s and '50s.* Toronto 1996.
Wilkins, Russell. *L'espérance de vie par Quartier à Montréal 1976* Apr. 1979. HB

1360M6E5 Inst. for Res. on Public Policy. 3535 Q. suite #514.
Woodley, E.C. *The House of Joseph in the Life of Quebec* Quebec 1946.
Yelin, Shulamis. *Shulamis: Stories from a Montreal childhood*. 1983. FC 2947.25 Y44 A3.
Revue de Géographie de Montréal. G1 R42.

PART II
JUDAISMS

CHAPTER 4

WORLD

It could be said that the Jews, over the centuries, have been a peripatetic group.

In 1928, in the name of experimentation, Stalin cavalierly created the Jewish Autonomous District (Birobidjan) in Siberia, 900 miles north of Vladivostok, beside the Amur River. Here, the Jews were to have freedom of their religion, schools and cultures, but increasing repression held this in check. Only 22, 000 Jews were living there in 1990. Between 1990 and 1995, the Russians again have allowed new Yiddish and Hebrew schools and four new synagogues, but the Jews are leaving for Israel and the West. By 1995 only 10,000 Birobidjan Jews were left.[1] That's one story.

Vilnus, in Lithuania, was known as the "Jerusalem of the North," and scholars gravitated to the many libraries containing manuscripts and books in Yiddish collected there over the centuries. In 1939, Russia took Lithuania from Poland. In 1940, Germany took Lithuania from Russia and eliminated most of the Jewish population of 67,000. There are now 13,000 Vilnus Jews. This is another historical story.

There are thousands of stories that can be told by the total population of world Jewry. Which was, in 1993, 12,963,000. Israel was home to 4,335,200 while the rest, 8,527,800, lived elsewhere, in diaspora.[2]

Table 8: Jewish World Population through the Ages (000')

	1700	1800	1900	1939	1950	1985	1993
Asia	130	300	280	350	170	35	24
Palestine/Israel	18	15	50	450	1130	3560	4335
Europe	700	2700	8580	9370	3380	2685	1958
N. Africa	170	240	280	520	570	15	9
S. Africa	15	15	75	115	145	130	101
Oceania	0	0	20	40	60	80	96
C. & S. America	10	17	35	420	630	445	433
N. America	11	27	1015	4700	5200	6010	6008
Total	1051	3314	10285	15965	11285	12966	12963

Gilbert & Felsel & AJYB 1939

Table 9: Countries with Jewish Population—1993 and late 1930's

Rank	Country	Late 1930's	1993 Population
1	U.S.A.	4,228,000	5,650,000
2	Israel	375,000	4,335,200
3	France	240,000	530,000
4	Russia*	-	410,000
5	Ukraine*	-	400,000
6	Canada	155,000	358,000
7	Great Britain	300,000	296,000
8	Argentina	260,000	210,000
9	Brazil	40,000	100,000
10	South Africa	95,000	98,000
11	Australia	24,000	91,000

* U.S.S.R. in 1930's = 2,612,000 and in early 1990's 1,150,000 before breakup of U.S.S.R. Late 1930's Statistics Friesel, p. 15-19.

Until the creation of Israel, Jews lived everywhere as a minority. They have often suffered: under 14th-century pogroms in the Germanic, Franco and English States; from the Iberian expulsions of 1492-7; because of the partitioning of Poland in the 18th Century; in the 1840 revolutions; during the Pale of Settlement in Russia and Poland, 1804-1881; in more pogroms in Eastern Europe, 1882-1917 (the result being mass migration westward); from the loss of rights in Rumania in 1881 and 1919; in the horrific Holocaust, 1933-1945; during the emigration of Jews from Arab lands after 1948; and, most recently, during the Russian Jews' migration of the 1970-1990s.

The changes are dramatically shown in Tables #9, #10, and #15, especially in Poland, where there were 3,029,000 in the late 1930s, and now only a total of 3,500.

Table 10: European Countries—1930's and 1993.

Country	Late 1930's	1993 Population
Hungary	443,000	55,000
Germany	449,500	52,000
Belarus	*	40,700
Belgium	60,000	31,800
Italy	47,800	31,200
Netherlands	156,800	25,500
Switzerland	18,000	18,000
Latvia	93,000	17,000
Lithuania	155,000	16,000
Sweden	6,700	15,000
Rumania	98,400	15,000
Moldova	*	15,000
Spain/Portugal	4,000	12,000
Czech. Rep./Slovakia	356,800	7,600
Austria	191,400	7,500
Greece	73,000	4,800
Poland	3,029,000	3,500
Estonia	4,000	3,200
Yugoslavia (old)	68,400	3,200
Bulgaria	77,000	1,700

* part of USSR
JYB 1996, and Friesel

A list of major cities with substantial Jewish population is in the appendix. Each city experienced major demographic change. For instance, Salonika, Greece, where the distressing forces of the Holocaust changed its face, was in the 1930s a thriving city with 55,000 Jews making up of 23% of the population. In 1992, 1000 dwelled there. In Israel, in 1995 with a population of 4,335,200 Jews, out of a total 5,328,000, there have been many shifts in the makeup of the population. Diverse religions, languages, original countries' customs, and modern socio-political themes have made Israel a real melting-pot as people from the Diaspora have swelled the population.

Table 11: Jews in Israel—1988

Origin	Foreign Born	Israel Born	Total
Asia	278,800	468,700	747,500
Africa	322,500	471,500	794,000
Asia/Africa total			1,441,500
Euro-American	741,800	1,589,400	2,331,200
AJYB—1990			3,772,7000

Table 12: U.S.A. Jewish Population 1878-1990

		% of Pop.
1878	229,600	0.5
1927	4,228,200	3.6
1986	5,814,300	2.5
1990	5,981,000	2.4

AJYB—1995

Notes

1. *Economist.* "Jerusalem on the Amur", May 6 1995, p.52.
2. A.J.Y.B. '95

References

Bachi, Roberto. *Population Trends of World Jewry*. Jerusalem, 1976. DS 140 B32. Inst. of Contemporary Jewry Hebrew U. of Jerusalem.

Cohen, S.M. *Perspectives in Jewish Population Research* Boulder, Colo. 1984. DS 143 P. 467. Important Tables

Huntington, Samuel P. *The Clash of Civilization and the remaking of World Order.* N.Y. 1996. D860 H86

Keyfitz, Nathan. *World People Growth & Aging*. Chicago 1990. HA155 K49.

Lerman, A. (ed.) et al. *The Jewish Communities of the World* (4th ed.) London, 1989. Ref. McL. DS 143 J49. (Inst. of Jewish Affairs).

Pascal, Julia. *Vanishing Diaspora: The Jews in Europe Since 1945*. London, 1995.

Schmelz, V. O., Della Pergola S. & Auner, U. "Ethnic differences among Israeli: Jews: a new look." *AJYB*, 1990: 3,5 & 128-31.

Schmelz V.O., Glikor, P. & Gould, S.J., *Studies in Jewish Demography* survey for 1972-1980. Jerusalem, 1983. DS 143 S77. See p. 1-17.

Schmelz, V.O. "Jewish Survival: The Demographic Factors." *Am J.Y.B.* 1981 p. 61-117.

Schmelz, V.O. (editor) "Demography & Statistics of Diaspora Jewry 1920-1970 Bibliography", *Inst. of Contemporary Jewry*, Jerusalem, 1976. Z6366 J52.

Schmelz, V.O. t al. (ed.) *Papers in Jewish Demography* World Congress of Jewish Studies. World Congress of Jewish Studies (7th Congress 1977) Jerusalem 1977. Inst. of Contemporary Jewry 1980. DS 140 W67 1977

Stillman, Norman A. *The Jews of Arab Lands in Modern Times* Philadelphia, 1991. DS 135 A68575

Tobin, G. A. and Chenkin Alvin. "Recent Community Pop. Studies: A Roundup" *AJYB* 85 (1985) 154-178.

Weeks, John R. *Population on Introduction to Concepts and Issues* (6th ed.) Belma CD 1996. HB 871 W43

Economist. "Germany—Survivors" Jan. 20, 1996, p. 51.

Economist. "Jerusalem on the Amur", May 6, 1995, p.52.

Yearbooks and Atlas

The New Standard Jewish Encyclopedia. 7th Revised Edition. Wigoder, G. (Ed.) New York, 1992.

American Jewish Year Book 1995. Singer David (Ed.) N.Y. 1995.

Encyclopedia of Jewish Institutions. Rosen, O. (Editor) U.S. & Canada, Tel Aviv 1983. Ref E 184—J5E 53.

The Jewish Year Book 1995 Massic S.W. (ed.) London, 1995. DS 135E 5A3

The Jewish Year Book 1995 Massic S.W. (ed.) London, 1997. DS 135E 5A3

World Jewish Directory. Lipsitz, E.Y. (Editor). Downsview Ont. 1991. REF PS 102.9W67

Atlas of Modern Jewish History. Friesel, Evyatar (ed.). Oxford 1990. Folio G1030 F6513

Gilbert, Martin. *Jews in History*. 4th ed. G 103065 1992.

A Historical Atlas of the Jewish People. Eli Barnavi (ed.), N.Y. 1992.

Atlas of Jewish History. D. Cohn-Sherbok (ed.), London 1996.

CHAPTER 5

JUDAISM

Rabbi Charles Bender gave me the chance to discuss the various questions that had come up in my readings.

Though 93 years old in 1990, he was spry and had a very agile mind. He lived in an apartment in Outremont, with his sister. We quickly entered into a discussion on the Torah and its interpretations (Mishnah and Tosefta), which together make up the Talmud. He showed me copies written in the original Hebrew which he said he went back to read when he needed spiritual sustenance.

He talked of the more than 2000 weddings he had officiated in over the 62 years he had been in Montreal, and was justly proud in officiating a third generation wedding that month. He had been a Jewish "Padre" in the RCAF and a Jewish "Chaplain" at the St. Vincent de Paul Penitentiary. He was then directing a small group in Outremont—a shtiebl—that worships together as their parent synagogue had moved to Snowdon.

He thumbed through the Torah and came to a passage he felt I should remember—one that he felt concerned him in his life:"And that ye may teach the children of Israel all the statutes which the Lord hath spoken unto them by the hand of Moses" (Lev. 10:11).

I knew I had met a man whose Judaism was not so much a religion as it was a complete life. Here was a life devoted to a lifetime of wisdom. I was in awe.

Finally, late in the afternoon, I left.

Judaism

Judaism is not a religion in the narrow contemporary sense but a way of life. Benedictus Spinoza, in Ethics IV A.1, comments: "The greatest thing the mind can understand is God." He goes on to say: "I believe in one God and with perfect faith and charity in the coming of the Messiah". Parts of these two statements could be used to describe many faiths, but together they give the essence of Judaism.

The primary theological doctrines of Judaism are monotheism, creation, covenant, revelation, and redemption. All these doctrines parallel Christianity.

Judaism is a:
1. belief in one God
2. belief in the coming of the Messiah
3. belief in the Ten Commandments
4. belief in the strength and religiosity of the prophets
5. humanistic and positive approach to fellow human beings

Judaism differs from Christianity in that,
  A. for Christianity the Messiah has come
  B. the disciples of Jesus wrote about his wishes and actions
  C. Paul of Tarsus institutionalized the rudiments of hierarchial power in Christianity, later resulting, for instance, in the decree that in the Roman Catholic sect, the Pope became infallible,
  D. Christianity incorporates the negative feeling of sin.

The biblical writings on which Judaism is based are the first five books of the Old Testament (collectively the Pentateuch), the Books of the Prophets and Writings, (including the Psalms). These three treatises combine to form the Jewish Bible—the Tanakh.

The Torah is the instructive interpretative instrument for the teaching of Judaism and is highly revered. As in every aspect of life, in Judaism,there are different degrees of traditionalism and modernism. The Torah is a God-revealed writing to the traditionalist, while the modernists feel that the Torah shapes their judgemental process and informs their reason and experience.

The same can be said for the Mishnah, a body of writings of experiences and interpretations of the Torah, and the Tosefta, supplemental material written by scholars throughout the ages, which, with the Torah, make up the Talmud. The Talmud can be said to contain the acculmated wisdom of the Jewish people.

Judaism has had no supreme commander. Jewish pluralism has resulted in a diversity of practice. From Palestinian and Babylonian Judaisms, there have been successive adaptations to Hellenism, Zoroastrianism, Romanism, Christianity, and lastly, Islam. Outside the Middle East, because of isolation or migration, the basic concepts of Judaism were practised but were adjusted to the new cultural and linguistic groups encountered.

However, there is some standardization of the practice of Judaism:

1 **Prayer**: a bridge between man and God
2 **Eating** (Kashrut = dietary practices)
   - Kosher prescriptions
   - rites of the table
3 **Festivals and Holidays**—"The Sacred Rand"
   Sabbath, practised:
   - Friday sundown to Saturday sundown
   - at home · best clothes
     - lighting of candles at Friday sundown
     - kiddush—prayer
     - festive meals and talk

- restoration of vigor of Judaism and its group.

Rosh Hashanah—New Year, beginning of the Hebrew calendar year, usually in September
- Reaffirmation of the sovereignty of God
- a quest for the regeneration of the Jewish heart

Yom Kippur—Day of Atonement, dusk to dusk.
- a solemn fast
- seeking regeneration

Sukkoth (Tabernacles) 8 days of harvest celebration
- reading Torah
- building a Succah at back of the dwelling.

Passover (Pesah)—advent of springtime
- liberation of Jews from Egypt

Hanukkah—Festival of lights Victory of Maccabees
- the cause of freedom of conscience

Purim—the day of lots
- deliverance from Haman

Tish A' B'ab—9th day of Month of Ab.
- mourning of the destruction of the first and second temples of Jerusalem

4 **Rites**—Life Cycle
Birth
- circumcision
- naming
- redemption of the first born

Education
- Bar/Bat Mitzvah
  calling to the Torah

Wedding
- solemnization of Betrothal
- marriage
- doorpost mezuzah

Death
- confession
- tearing of garment in token of bereavement (Keriah)
- kaddish—mourner's prayer

5 Institutions

A Jew can pray at any time but a prerequisite for formal worship is to have a quorum of 10 adults above thirteen (Orthodox —10 male adults) which is called a Minyan.

The synagogue is the house of prayer and of study, and a meeting place for the congregation. Many schools and associations are attached to and use the synagogue.

Each congregation is autonomous and is guided by a tradition dictated by a Board of Directors and an appointed Rabbi. Helping, is a Cantor who leads the Sabbath prayers and worship, reads the Torah and teaches youth (a Cantor is not ordained like the Rabbi).

To attain the Rabbinate, a person must, after years of private or academic study [Yeshiva], get a certificate of ordination. The Rabbi derives his livelihood from his ability to teach the tradition dictated by the congregation. Rabbis have a great deal of independence. There is a shortage of Rabbis of all sects in Canada. Most Rabbis in Montreal come from the United States.

Past History of Judaism starting at the 12th Century—their Rights and Migrations

By the 12th Century, due to the course of commerce and migration, the Jews had spread throughout Western Europe. Under Roman Catholic domination in France, Germany, and England, under Eastern Orthodoxy in Russia and the Balkans, and under Islamic rule in the Iberian Peninsula, Jews were always a subjugated minority clinging to their tradition.

In 1215, the Fourth Latenan Council established an elaborate anti-Jewish code of laws culminating in the expulsion of Jews from England in 1290, and later between 1305-94, from German and Italian cities between 1400-1500, and from the Iberian peninsula in the1490s. The European Jews moved eastward into isolation in Poland, Lithuania, Russia, and bordering countries, while the Iberian Jews travelled to the lands of the Mediterranean, the port cities of the Low Countries, and the Americas. The Iberian Jews became the majority of the Palestinian Jews in the 16th century.

In Eastern Europe, always hoping for salvation from their under-privileged lot and their stagnating isolation, the communities looked to their learned leaders—their Rabbis—to lead them to a better world. Baal Shem Tov (Besht), in the 18th century, helped create a concept of the Rabbi as the spiritual guide of the community and founded Hasidism. At the same time (1772), Russia started to annex parts of Poland (completing the annexation by 1795). Russia instituted prohibitions against the Jews in 1804 with the concept of the 'Pale of Settlement', ghettoizing the Jews. Russian Jews had to wait for the Russian Revolution in 1917 to get their rights.

In Western Europe, Napoleon allowed Jews full citizenship in France in 1791; emancipation of the Jews occurred in England by 1858; in Austro-Hungary by 1867; and in Germany by 1871.

In contrast, in Canada Jews obtained full rights in 1832.

During the mid 19th century, influenced by the Protestant successes in Germany, the modernistic Jews formed a liberal Reform movement in 1850. The Conservative movement was formed in 1890 due to many feeling that the Reform movement had become too liberal and that Judaism needed more traditional values but not the isolationistic Orthodox concepts.

Meanwhile, the Iberian Jews had spread over the Mediterranean, England, the Netherlands, and outposts of

South and North America, retaining their Orthodoxy and their cultural traditions. Their settlements were quite stable and they were usually in port cities, so they were able to contact the outside world—unlike their European brethren, many of whom were still situated in isolated communities.

The general mood in Russia after 1880 was a heightening of anti-semitism manifested as pogroms, boycotts, quotas, newspaper and pamphlet attacks, riots and charges of ritual murder. The pamphlet tract, The Protocols of the Elders of Zion—1905, helped radicalize the people against the Jews. With five million Jews in Russia in 1897, emigration increased. Most Jews opted for the "golden streets" of America. However, visions of Canada's law and order and lots of land brought many immigrants to this country.

Another vision appeared, Zionism, that decreed the re-establishment of the land of Israel as the center of a new Jewish life in Palestine, which at that time (the 1870s) had a Jewish population of 24,000. The First Aliyah (wave of return) was started by the Bilu Association of Kharko during the Russian pogroms of 1881-82. In 1897, the First World Zionist Congress was held in Basle and the ideas of Zionism were solidified into a credo—one must return from Diaspora to create a new and strong homeland.

By 1900, America was on the mind of everyone who was unsettled or poor. The internal pressures of the states of Eastern Europe on the Jews there helped their emigration. The wealthy and relatively assimilated Jews of Western Europe didn't want to be aligned with these linguistically foreign Jews. These Western Jews—(pseudo-proto Zionists) pressured European governments, especially the British, to encourage many of these Jews to go to Palestine. Also, the need for non-Arab people to swell the population in the Palestine Mandate lands was another factor that inspired emigration.

In 1917, Lord Arthur James Balfour, a powerhouse in British Conservative ranks for 40 years, in his capacity as Foreign

Secretary, under pressure by Zionists Nahum Sokolow and Chaim Weizman, wrote a letter to Baron Rothchild. This letter was a great impetus for the establishment of the State of Israel.

References

Arnold, Abraham. *Judaism: Myth, Legend, History and Custom From the Religious to the Secular.* Montreal, 1995.

Elbolm-Dror, Rachel."Herzl's radical vision changed World history" C.J.N. Feb 15 '96 p.9.

Kahan, Arcadins. *Essays on Jewish Social and Economic History.* Chic 1986, DS1405K33

Kahane, Rabbi Meir. *Why Be Jewish?* N.Y. 1977. D.S. 143K26

Koestler, A. *The Thirteenth Tribe: The Kazar Empire and Its Heritage.* London, 1976. DK 34K45K5. DK 509D8

Landau, David. *Diety and Power: The World of Jewish Fundamentalism.* N.T. 1993. BM 198 L26

Meyer, Michael A. *Jewish Identity in the Modern World.* Settle 1990. DS143M39.

Raphael, Chaim. *The Road from Babylon.* London, 1985. DS135S7R36.

Reinharz, Jehuda. "The Balfour Declaration in Historical Perspective"p. 587-616 in *Essential Papers on Zionism,* Reinharz, Jehuda and Shapira, Anita (editors) New York 1996 DS149E76.

Rome, David. "5000 Years of Jewish Identity." Monchanin 20, 3: 96: 2-16.

Rosenberg, Stuart, E. "What Christians don't know about Judaism". C.J. Congress, Montreal, 1964.

Rosenthal, Gilbert. "Messianism Reconsidered". Judaism 40 #4 fall 91: 552-568.

Roth, Cecil. *A Short History of Jewish People.* London, 1969. DS118 R6 19696

Scholem, G. G. *Major Trends in Jewish Mysticism.* N.Y. 1954.

Schwarz, Leo, W. (Ed.) *Great Ages and Ideas of the Jewish People.* N.Y. 1956.

Seltzer, R. M. *Jewish People Jewish Thought.* N.Y. 1980. 874 pages. Superb maps.

Sigal, Phillip. *Judaism: The Evolution of a Faith.* Grand Rapids,1988. BM 155.2.S47. Excellent glossary.

Sklare, Marshell (Ed.) *American Jews—A Reader.* N.Y. 1983.

    On Reform Judaism "Reform is a Verb" p. 275-300 Leonard S. Fein et al.

    On Orthodoxy "Orthodoxy in American Jewish Life," p. 319-364. Charles S. Liebman

Sklare, Marshall, (Ed.) *The Jews: Social Patterns of an American Group.* Glencoe, 1958.

Steinberg, Milton. *Basic Judaism.* N.Y., 1947.

Foreign Office,
November 2nd, 1917.

Dear Lord Rothschild,

I have much pleasure in conveying to you, on behalf of His Majesty's Government, the following declaration of sympathy with Jewish Zionist aspirations which has been submitted to, and approved by, the Cabinet

"His Majesty's Government view with favour the establishment in Palestine of a national home for the Jewish people, and will use their best endeavours to facilitate the achievement of this object, it being clearly understood that nothing shall be done which may prejudice the civil and religious rights of existing non-Jewish communities in Palestine, or the rights and political status enjoyed by Jews in any other country"

I should be grateful if you would bring this declaration to the knowledge of the Zionist Federation.

CHAPTER 6

MEDITERRANEAN AND EUROPEAN JEWS

A sect is defined (in the Oxford English Dictionary) as a separate group adhering to a distinctive doctrine or way of thinking, or to a particular leader, or to both. Within Judaism, there are two main sects—Sephardim and Ashkenazim.

The Jews of the Iberian Peninsula, isolated from the European Jews and given rights under their Moorish masters, evolved into Sephardim. Incorporating the Moorish customs and combining Hebrew with Spanish to fashion the dialect Ladino, the Sephardim continued to adhere to the Orthodox faith of Judaism. After the reconquest of the Iberian Peninsula by Roman Catholic forces, the Jews retained their rights until the late 15th century.

In Europe, strict Roman Catholicism kept the Jews in isolation by forbidding them to move from their city or town. Until the 17th century, all groups sought to preserve and continue their tradition and turned to their leaders in each location or synagogue for leadership. This then created new sub-sects of Ashkenazim, which were courts of Orthodoxy headed by a Rabbi having his own interpretations of the Torah.

N.A. Stillman, in a talk at Montreal's Jewish Public Library on May 19, 1992, separated the and identified main cultural and religious differences.

Table 13: Simple Differences—Ashkenazim vs. Sephardim

	Orthodox Ashkenazim	Sephardim
Climate	Closed buildings Cold area of Europe	Open courtyards of the Mediterranean
Religious Tolerance	Persecution by R.C. and Protestant	Islam having Hellenistic secular tradition
Clothing	Black	colourful
Jobs	restricted to the ones no one wanted- e.g. money lending & tax collection	No restriction become artisans and craftsmen
Travel	restricted pale of settlement ghetto	no restriction
Religion	very decorative	very decorative, derived from Arabic culture
Place of worship	Catholic influence	Arabic influence

N.A. Stillman

Ashkenazis outnumbered Sephardics everywhere except France and Israel in the 1980s. One presumes the balance is shifting in Israel with the influx of Russian Jews.

Table 14: Jews in the World (1984)

Diaspora	Ashkenazim	Sephardim	Total
Canada	290	35	325
U.S.A.	5502	185	5692
Lat. Am.	404	50	454
France	230	300	530
West Europe	469	50	519
East. Europe & Turkey	1590	120	1710
Asia	2	35	37
N. Africa	0	17	17
S. Africa	126	5	131
Oceania	93	2	95
Total	8706	799	9505
Israel	1672	1800	3472
Grand Total	10378	2599	12977

Cohen, and Schmelz.

References

Bachi, Roberto. *Population Trends of World Jews.* Jerusalem, 1976. DS 140 B32

Cohen, Steven M. et al. (ed.) *Perspectives in Jewish Population Research.* Boulder, 1984. DS 143 P467

Schmelz, V.O. et al. (ed.) *Studies in Jewish Demography.* New York, 1983.

Zimmels, H.L. *Ashkenazim and Sephardim* London, 1958, BM 182.Z5

CHAPTER 7

SEPHARDIM

On March 31, 1492, "Ferdinard II of Aragon and Isabella I of Castile signed a decree that gave the Jews four months to leave Spain"[1]. Up to 100,000 left, calling themselves Sephardim (Hebrew name for Spain being Sepharad). Great numbers went to the eastern Mediterranean under Ottoman rule and to North African countries that were under Arab rule. Others settled in Italy, southern France, and the ports of the Low Countries—areas of Roman Catholic and Protestant influence. The Jews that stayed had to convert to Roman Catholicism though many continued to practice their Judaism secretly—these were called Marranos. Five years later, in Portugal, the Jews were banished, when Princess Isabel of Castile married Portugal's King Manuel.

At the end of the 17th century, there were concentrations of Sephardim in Fez, Tunis, Alexandra, Damascus, Smyrna, Salonika, and Constantinople. Smaller communities were in Amsterdam, Venice and London.

As the Western European powers started imposing their colonial aspirations on the weaker states, the Treaty of Berlin of 1878 carved up Africa. The Young Turk revolution of 1908— the final blow against the Ottomans—opened up the Middle East to colonization.

The surviving Sephardim then prospered in each location until World War II during which the Fascists and Nazis deported whole communities to the death camps. For example, on Rhodes, 2000 of 2200 Sephardim went to the camps. After World War II, with the formation of the state of Israel in 1948, the Jews in any Arab country were at risk, and began to emigrate en masse. For example, in Algeria, 130,000 Jews wanted to retain their French citizenship. Most Jews feared that after Algeria became an independent Arab State, they might be held as hostages in the event of a new Arab-Israeli war. At Independence, July 1, 1962, 13,000 had gone to Israel, 109,000 to France and 13,000 had stayed.[2] In 1986, however, none were left.

Table 15: Jews in Islamic Countries

Countries	Before 1948	1986	1994	
Morocco	230,000	12,000	8,000	Casablanca, Fez & Rabat
Algeria	130,000	1,500	0	
Tunisia	85,000	3,000	2,400	in Tunis ('95 = 1500)
Libya	40,000	0	0	
Egypt	66,000	300	200	
Yemen	52,000	1,000	500	
Turkey	80,000	20,000	20,000	in Istanbul
Syria	30,000	4,000	3,000	by 1996 = 300
Lebanon	5,000	0	0	
Iraq	125,000	200	0	
Iran	90,000	22,000	10,000	in Tehran
Afghanistan	5,000	0	0	

Friesel, p. 76

Notes

1. Diaz-Mas, Paloma. *Sephardim, The Jews from Spain*. Chicago, 1992. DS 134 D52413
2. Henissart, Paul. *Wolves in the City—Death of French Algeria*. N.Y., 1970. p.346.

References

Allan Richard. *Imperialism and Nationalism in the Fertile Crescent*. N.Y., 1974.

Berbaruk, Salomon. *Trois-Quarts de Siècle Pêle-Mêle: Maroc-Canada 1920-50-90.* FC 2950J5 B45 Montreal 1990

Diaz-Mas, Paloma. *Sephardim, The Jews from Spain*. Chicago, 1992. DS 134 D52413

Dobrinsky, Herbert. (V.P. of University Affairs Yeshiva University, N.Y. N.Y.) *A Treasury of Sephardic Laws & Customs*. N.Y., 1986. MM700D56

Elazar, Daniel Judah. *The Other Jews: The Sephardic Today*. N.Y., 1980 DS 134E4

Elazar, Daniel. "Can Sephardic Judaism be Reconstructed?" *Judaism* 41(3) June 92, 217-228.

Haim, S. "First Arab Student Congress, Brussels 1938". From *Arab Nationalism: An Anthology*. Sylvia Haim (ed.) Berkeley, 1962.p.100-102

Henissart, Paul. *Wolves in the City—Death of French Algeria*. N.Y., 1970.

Kedourie, Elie. *Spain and the Jews: The Sephardim Experience—1492 and After*. London, 1992. DS 135 S7S62

Laskier, Michael. *North African Jewry in the 20th Century*. N.Y. 1994.DS135A25L36

Lewis, Bernard. *Jews of Islam*. Princeton 1984. PB173J8L48

Netanyahu, Benzion. *The Origins of the Inquisition in 15th Century Spain*. New York, 1995.

Papo, Joseph M. *Sephardim in 20th Century America: In Search of Unity*. San Jose, CA, 1987.

Stillman, Norman A. *The Jews of Arab Lands in Modern Times*. Phila., 1991. DS135A68S75.

CHAPTER 8

ASHKENAZIM

The majority of the Ashkenazi Jews populated France, Germany, Central Europe, and European Russia at the time of the emergence of Protestantism. The Jews in Western Europe enjoyed the freedom to air intellectual and political opinion and discover new areas for their new trades due to the coming of the Age of Reason. Now, not necessarily dictated to by their Rabbis, they reexamined their positions on Judaism.

1. **Orthodoxy**
In the East, unable to emigrate and shaken by exterminations such as the Chmielniki Cossack massacres in south Poland and the Ukraine, between 1648 and 1656, the pogroms of the Pale of Settlement, the machinations of messianic fanatics preying on the superstitious people who lived in isolation, and the lack of education (except for their Rabbis), these Orthodox Jews needed a relief from their hard existence. In the Hasidic Movement, they found a sect that rebuilt their faith—a rejoicing in serving God (spelt G-D so that if each printed letter was either destroyed by burning or thrown away, the word of God would not be extinguished). Hasidism was created by shifting the focus:

    1. from from strictly talmudic opinions to esoteric, joyous opinions.

2. **from** discussion and speculation on the meanings in religious study **to** the preoccupation with exactitude (fixed formulas) in ritual.
3. **from** the quiet confidence in God's response to the Jewish ideals **to** an effort to compel God's response with more exactitudes.

Each town and surrounding area had its Rabbi or a learned man who everyone looked up to for decisions. These famous men gathered others around them and formed 'courts' where they learned to read and write and discuss all aspects of Judaism.

There were opponents to Hasidim. The Mitnagdim, mainly in Lithuania, continued to be Orthodox. But soon Hasidim infiltrated all of Eastern Europe and weakened this movement. In Hungary, another center of Ultra-Orthodoxy arose—the Hatam Sofar. "The new is forbidden by the Torah" was their rallying cry. The Hatam didn't reject the new emancipation of the West, but felt it was a mixed blessing. The Hatam believed that the West's ideas shouldn't change the Orthodox in their closeness to God and in their belief of a Messiah.

By the mid-19th century, there was a distinct difference between the isolated communities in the East and the more highly educated and richer Western Jews.

Issues that divide orthodoxy:
a. attitude toward general knowledge differs within Orthodoxy
b. role of women
c. availability of education for children
d. authority of writings in non-legal matters by the Rabbinate
e. attitude toward the non-Jewish society. The ultra-Orthodox excludes the non-Jews from equality in

God's eyes and tries to sever its connection with the non-Jewish society

f. to the Orthodox Jews, the term 'State of Israel' is a Zionist term and they are against non-religious Zionists whom they feel are not G-d-fearing.

g. attitude toward non-Orthodox Jews. To the Ultra Orthodox "any individual Jew is equally a Jew with any other, nevertheless, the ultra Orthodox have taken the position that it is not appropriate for Orthodoxy, in any way, to recognize the legitimacy of any form of Judaism such as Reform, Conservatives, Reconstructionist . . . and Zionism."[1]

In the contemporary world, there are parallels in other religions. For example, when visiting Amish county, in Pennsylvania, I found that modern dress is forbidden, and only black is worn—men wear black hats and women long skirts, similar to the Ultra-Orthodox Jew. In education, however, the Amish are stricter—allowing no education after the ninth grade on penalty of being expelled from the community. In Mahfouz's *Palace Walk*, a novel about an Egyptian Islamic family, the male head of the family allows the women of the family little contact with the outside world.

The Ultra-Orthodox needs to defend him or herself not just from the gentile society but also from the intrusion of the less traditional Jewish society: "Hasidic Jews live outside the walled town but they want the wall to be there".[2]

Table 16: Ashkenazi Judaism: differences between West and East

	West
A. Orthodoxy	
1. General framework	Westernized Ashkenazic
2. Leadership	Accent on achieved qualities of scholarship and rhetorical skill which are subject to rational evaluation; mastery of local vernacular is essential
3. Synagogue behaviour	Formal, quiet, and orderly; sermons in vernacular
4. Community	Good local organization
5. Attitude toward secular learning	Permissive
6. Spoken language	Local vernacular
7. Outward appearance	Western urban
8. Occupations	All middle-class occupations
B. Non-Orthodox Elements	
1. General nature	Through and partial reform; the latter (Historical Judaism) became main force behind study of Jewish history and archaeology
2. Community	Weak congregational organization; no true community to speak of
3. Spoken language	Local vernacular
C. General Characteristics (cutting across split between Orthodox and non-Orthodox)	
1. Attitude toward time	Western respect for punctuality
2. Economic aspects	
a. general picture	Sound
b. business practice	Western-style orderly practices
3. Cleanliness	Meticulous
4. Manners	Restrained mode of speech; general "good manners" as defined in the West

Rubin, p. 26-27

Table 16: (Continued)
East (except Lithuania)
A.
1. Predominantly Hasidic
2. (a) Hasidic community: charismatic-traditional; important qualities are: pedigree and piety; scholarship is of secondary importance
   (b) Residential community: of primary importance are the qualities of scholarship and leadership ability, both rationally evaluated; oratorical skill is an asset but not a "must"; is, as a rule, secondary in importance to the Hasidic rebbeh
3. Informal, vociferous, individualized, and includes various unconventional activities
4. Potent Hasidic community superimposed on weak residential community
5. Negative

6. Yiddish
7. Beard, dark long coat buttoned right side on top of left, and white shirt
8. Middle-class occupations except liberal professions and white-collar work

B.
1. Enlightenment; accent on value of secular knowledge; attempt to create secular literature in Yiddish and Hebrew; no endeavor to create religious reform

2. No separate community; loose local community permitted their existence without organizational chasm

3. Mixture of Yiddish and vernacular

C.

1. Relaxed
2.
   a. Insecure
   b. Shrewdness, bargaining
3. No particular emphasis
4. Vociferousness; gesticulation; free display of emotions.

Realizing that the Hasidim would not discuss their precepts with me, I derived an anagram from my name—Yackam Mitsh— and wrote away to 3 Hasidic organizations and got their brochures and newsletters. Later, I went with Neil Caplan to a talk given by Alan Dershowitz at the Shaar Hashomayim. The hall was packed—even the front seats at $50 a piece. After the interesting speech there was a book signing and sale of Dershowitz's newest book. I had brought along one of his older books, *Chutzpah*, and waited in line. My turn arrived.

"Oh, *Chutzpah*—how would you like it dedicated?" he said.

"To Yackam, Y-A-C-K-A-M, please" I replied

As he wrote "To Yackam, my best" he said:" Yackam, a nice jewish name, seldom heard."

My smile hid my laughter, and chutzpah.

Notes

1. Berman, Rabbi S. "What is Orthodoxy" *Jewish Spectator* Summer 1990, p.15-17.
2. Beitel, Garry. Quote from the Minority and Media Symposium. McGill University, March 21, 1994, talking about his 'Bonjour, Shalom' film.

References

Abraham, Pearl. *The Romance Reader*. New York, 1995.

Beitel, Garry. Quote from the Minority and Media Symposium. McGill University, March 21, 1994, talking about his 'Bonjour, Shalom' film.

Berman, Rabbi S. "What is Orthodoxy" *Jewish Spectator* Summer 1990, p. 15-20.

Bloom, Bernand. "No on the Rebbe" *Jewish Spectator*, Summer 1990, p. 61.

Buber, Martin. *The Origin and Meaning of Hasidism*. N.Y., 1960. BM198 B843.

Buber, Martin. *Hasidism & Modern Man*. N.Y., 1958. BM 198 B793.

Chartrand, Luc "Juifs des pays" (TASH) *Actualité* 16 #70 (15 Dec. 91) p. 52-60. AP21A33X

Danzger, Herbert. *Returning to Tradition: The Contemporary Revival of Orthodox Judaism*. New Haven, 1989. BM 205 D27

Dershowitz, Alan M. *Chutzpah*. Toronto, 1991.

Fishkoff, Sue. "Tears of Faith" *Jerusalem Post* (int. Ed.). Jan. 29, 1994. p.10.

Garvin, Philip & Cohen Arthur A. *A People Apart* BM 198 G35 1970
Gorenberg, G. "The rebbe and the spaceship" *The Jerusalem Report* March 19, 1992.
Gutwirtz, Jacques. "The structure of a Hasidic Community in Montreal," *Jew J. of Soc.* 141 (June 1972) 43-62 DS101 J4657
Gutwirtz, Jacques. *Vie juive traditionnelle* Paris,1970. BM198 G83
Hostetler, John A. *Amish Society*. Baltimore, 1968. BX129 A6H6.
Mahfouz, Najib. *Palace Walk*, N.Y., 1990.
Margalit, Avishai, "Israel: The risk of the Ultra-Orthodox." *N.Y. Review of Books*, p. 38-44. Nov. 9, 1989.
Mitchner, James. *The Source*. N.Y. 1965. p. 680. PS 3525 I 1956
Papo, Eliezel. *Essential Pele Yoetz*. M. Angel (ed.) N.Y., 1991. BJ 1287 P363 P4513.
Rabinowicz, Haron M. *The World of Hasidism* London,1970. BM198 R28.
Regenstreif, M. *The Gazette* May, 21, 1992 article on Hasidim in interview with William Shaffir.
Rubin, Israel. *Satmar: An Island in the City*. Chicago, 1972. BM 198 R8
Schmeltz U.O. et al. "Ethnic differences among Israeli Jews: A new look." *Am J. Y. Book* 1990. E 184J5A6.
Shaffir, William "Separate from the Mainstream in Canada: The Hasidic Community of Tash" *Jew J. of Sociology* XXIX: 1: Jan. 1987: 19-35. McL DS 101 J4657
Shaffir, William. "Hasidic Jews & Quebec Politics". *Jew J. of Sociology* XXV: #2 Dec. 83, p. 105-118.
Shaffir, William. "Becoming an Orthodox Chassidic Jew: The Socialization of Newcomers to a Religious Community". *Can Ethnic Studies* Vol. VI, 1978, p. 295-309.
Shaffir, William. "Jewish Messianism Lubavitch-Style: An Interim Report." *Jew J. of Sociology*, v. 135, #2 Dec. 1993.
Zylberberg, Jacques et al. "De la mystique au pouvoir: étatisation et depolitisation de hassidim Montrealais". *Conférence Internationale de Sociologie des Religion: ACTES* 18 (1985) 221-26.
Gazette May 5, 1990. p.5.

2. Non Orthodox

"The pre-modern [read Orthodox] Jew, tightly circumscribed by social prejudice on the outside and religious belief on the inside, knew exactly where one stood in relation to both God and man, Jew and gentile. Beginning with the mid-18th century the gods of enlightenment, reason and universalism

Table 17: Some differences of rules and customs between Reform, Conservative and Orthodox.

		Reform
1.	Torah	Left wing modernists. Large changes in tradition on blind faith. Torah is God's revelation forever binding.
2.	Place of worship	Temple
3.	Language of worship	English
4.	Sound	Singing allowed
5.	Patrilineal descent	Yes
6.	during service men/women	sit together
7.	Commercialism	high
8.	covering of heads	sometimes
9.	Mitzvah	bar/bat
10.	non-Jews being accepted equally	Leans towards inter-faith meetings
11.	beliefs	varied interpretations of God
12.	Israel	committed to the survival of the state of Israel as a religious spiritual center
13.	Education	can have secular education
14.	Future	flux

Table 17: *(Continued)*

	Conservative	Orthodox
1.	Right wing modernist. Minimal changes in Torah seen as the culture of the Jewish people.	Total adherence to the historical prayer book. Divine origin of the Torah
2.	Synagogue	Synagogue or shul
3.	Some of liturgy in English	Hebrew only
4.	Instrumented music	no music
5.	Yes (sometimes no)	no
6.	sit together	segregated
7.	very high	no
8.	Yarmulke	hats
9.	bar/bat	bar (some bat)
10.	accept into faith only on theoretical level	no acceptance
11.	middle of the road approach	God is a personal deity
12.	Land of Israel is holy	Jewish people-God's Chosen. Restoration of the State of Israel along the lines of the Torah
13.	maximum Jewish education	parochial only
14.	trying to have a consensus or what is the middle of the road	constancy - other sects are merely contemporary fads and passing aberrations

shed those bonds, offering escape from the ghettos in exchange for the abandonment of the Orthodox faith."[3]

A more secular education and the exposure to the writings of Luther, Calvin and Zwingli caused many Jews in Western Europe to move away from Orthodoxy. According to Raphael, "the Reform Movement was an outgrowth of the universalistic hopes of the Enlightenment and especially of the hope that the differences between people would disappear".[4]

Recently, over the question and decision of women's ordination, the Conservatives have split into Conservative and Traditional Conservatives.

The Reconstructionist Movement was founded in 1922 by Mordecai Kaplan, breaking off from the Conservatives on the basic premise that Judaism is part of a "developing civilization".[5]

Unlike Orthodoxy, which had its rules and law dictated by the Torah and Talmud, the non-Orthodox sects openly discuss and challenge their concepts of their religion. This basic difference has opened up a chasm between the Orthodox and the more modern sects.

Maurice Cohen founded the Board of Jewish Ministers of Montreal, which included every English-speaking Rabbi in town. Today the organization is shunned by a number of young Orthodox rabbis who do not want to fraternize with Rabbis of other traditions.[6]

Notes

3. Economist, Nov. 9, 1991. p.104.
4. Raphael, Marc Lee. *Profiles in American Judaism* Cambridge May 1984. BM 197 R33. p.79.
5. Kaplan, Mordercai. *Judaism as a Civilization* Philadelphia 1981. BM 197.7 K26. p.11.
6. Gazette May 5, 1990. p.5.

References

Brown, Michael. "The Beginnings of Reform Judaism in Canada" *Jew Soc. St.* 34, 1972. p. 322-342.

Kaplan, Mordercai. *Judaism as a Civilization* Philadelphia 1981. BM 197.7 K26.

Raphael, Marc Lee. *Profiles in American Judaism* Cambridge May 1984. BM 197 R33

Rosenthal, Gilbert S. *Contemporary Judaism: Patterns of Survival* (2nd ed.) N.Y. 1986. BM 205R59

Temkin, Sefton D. "How Reform Judaism Developed" *Judaism* vol. 40 # 3, Jun. '91, 369-377.

Economist, Nov. 9, 1991. p.104.

3. Secular Judaism

In the West, the French Revolution introduced the logic of democratic principles, whereas in the past feudalism had dominated. The Revolution gave the Jews their emancipation in 1792, "not through a fraternal feeling for the Jews, but because logic demanded it. Popular sentiment rebelled but the philosophy of the Revolution decreed that principles must be placed higher than sentiment".[7]

In the rush to modernity, many Western Jews, having abandoned Orthodoxy and the ghetto to gain economic and cultural equality, left their roots. When the backlash (when sentiment overcame principles) occurred in the mid-1800's, many Jews were left doubly alienated—cut off from their roots and denied acceptance in the dominant Christian society once more.

The Jews who had rejected religion but continued to be Jewish secularists had many shades. For instance, the Marxists wanted to improve society by resolving inequities in the world; the atheists had a spiritual protest against the containment of God in the concepts and institutions of a limited religious movement; the secular Zionists had an ideal of a Jewish people in a Jewish land without the constraints of a fundamentalistic religion; there were also socialists, laborites, and humanists.

As an ideology, Jewish secularism presupposes at least some Jewish self-knowledge, and therefore cannot be traditionless. In fact, their "humanitarian concern for mankind is fully compatible with and even strengthened by an explicit Jewish identification".[8] Rav Kook, describing the difference between knowledgeable secularists and those who were 'non-Jewish' Jews, used the expressions "higher chutzpah" for those who had a principled rebellion against religion, and "lower chutzpah" for those sloughers who were ignorant, indifferent and purely self-centered.[9]

Zionism is surely a higher chutzpah. In the 19th Century, Zionism was born in Eastern Europe. The 'Land of Israel' was the quest, a hope for deliverance from the external oppression of the Christians and from the internal overpowering Rabbis. Making Aliyah—returning to Israel, a Jewish place, irrespective of how deep one's roots were in another community—energized many Jews. The idea of no longer wandering in Diaspora soon had adherents in the West. This was an important shift for the Zionist movement, because in order for Israel to be strong, it was necessary to have the support of Diasporic Jews.

Zionist theory today is that Jewish identity is essentially national and that Israel is the guarantee for the continuance of Judaism. No assimilation outside Israel is possible, and the liberal world must be somehow moved to act on the behalf of the restoration to the Jews of their rightful land.

In the late-19th and early-20th Centuries, sites such as Uganda were suggested. Most diplomats felt that the geographic location of Palestine was only on the edge of the western sphere of influence and in the midst of a people who were Islamic and would dislike another power and religion in their midst. But Zionists wanting to set up a state of Israel and religious Jews wanting to return to their many religious sites and traditions, lobbied to attain their aims.

In the political arena, 1917 was the turning point for

Zionism and all Jews' national rights in Palestine. Jews were worried that gaining these rights would jeopardize Jews in other countries in the matter of their receiving equal rights in the nations where they lived. Also, "many feared that the emergence of a secular Jewish state would completely obliterate the religious quality of Jewish life in Diaspora by [the new Jewish State] absorbing the major share of (world wide) Jewish money, time and effort".[10] In 1917, Kerensky brought Jews into his government in Russia. Britain, wanting to keep Russia in the war and encourage North American Jewry to back Britain in World War I, tried to appease the North American Jews by fostering ties with Zionism. According to Khouri, Britain was "encouraged by Zionist arguments that a Jewish-dominated Palestine would strengthen the British strategic position in the Middle East" (especially the new Suez Canal), and, "in addition, [they] hoped to use Zionist support to help block the internationalization of Palestine, as required by the secret Sykes-Pico Agreement with France, and thereby to obtain Palestine for Britain alone".[11]

The result was the Balfour Declaration, which led to Jewish territorial, political, social and cultural autonomy.

The Sephardic Jews believe in the same messianic hope of redemption as do the Ashkenazi. The individual tradition of aliyah contributed to large Sephardic communities in Jerusalem, Haifa, and Jaffa. There was also a group migration of the Yemenites to Palestine, starting in 1891, who were escaping their harsh conditions.

North American Jewry was split in its outlook on Zionism. The early interest was strong in Canada. There was no umbrella organization in Canada because the Jewish communities were spread throughout Canada. The flow of Eastern Europeans and their Zionist adherents into these communities finally created the Federation of Zionist Societies (in 1919, just before the Canadian Jewish Congress was formed). Unable to feel at home due to the vitriolic anti-semitism between the wars, the Zionists in Quebec were continuously given the needed push toward thoughts of a homeland. Later, in addition, there was the large population of Holocaust survivors and their families settled in Montreal who favoured a strong connection with Israel.

Today, Zionism has splintered again into many shades. There is even religious Zionism: the Mizrah movement which reaffirms its faith in a homeland, in their people and their traditions, is also called Torah Zionism or Orthodox Zionism. But Zionist ideology has not moved away from its pre-state views of the factual basis of its geographic concept of Israel. No theoretical thinkers have appeared since Herzl or Rav Reiner; and Zionism is now a "political football".

Zionism offers Jews from the Ultra Orthodox to the Reform to the Sephardim a national liberation movement—not just a faith—a sense of belonging. But some ultra-Orthodox attack Zionism in Israel for political purposes, while in North America the attack is to protect their own turf and make their flock realize there are "outside" threats within Judaism.

These battles within Judaism always have been prevalent. They were not just sect vs. sect but established groups versus incoming immigrants— geographically close but verbally and spiritually far apart.

Between World War I and World War II, Zionism flourished. Groups such as the Revisionist, Labonites, and Left —made up of the Poalei Zion, Communists, and Right wing parties of Anarchists and Bundists—were for the Jewish state.

Dissidents were everywhere, undermining the overall strength of the Jewish community. Some say that "It was Zionism [by later provoking British restrictions on entry into their Mandate —Palestine] that prevented many Jews like us from immigrating to the Land of Israel and this caused their death in the Nazi gas chambers".[12]

With the creation of the State of Israel in 1948, dissent became inadmissible. The world community of Judaism at this point stood together.

Notes

7. Nordau, Max. "On the situation of the Jews throughout the world." - 1897. From *The Jubilee of the First Zionist Congress 1897-1947*. Jerusalem, 1947. DS149A4Z5. p.57.
8. Schwartz (ed.) *The Menorah Treasury*. Philadelphia 1964. p.72.
9. Kook, Rav. *The Essential Writings of A.I. Kook*. N.Y. 1988. BM45 K646. p.
10. Greenstein, Howard. *Turning Point: Zionism and Reform Judaism*. Ann Anbor, 1981. BM 197 G72. p.82.
11. Khouri, T. J. *Arab-Israeli Dilemma* Syracuse 1968. p.5.
12. Margalit, Avishai. "Israel: The Rise of the Ultra Orthodox" *N.Y. Review of Books*. Nov. 9, 1989, p. 38.

References

Abella, Irving. "Dissent and Pluralism in the Montreal Jewish Community: A Historical Survey" *Viewpoints*, vol. XVI, #2 1988, p. 1-3.

Baldwin, James. "... the most difficult (and most rewarding) thing in my life has been the fact I was born a Negro and was forced, therefore, to effect some kind of truce with this reality" From *Turn To The South*, V.S. Naipaul, p. 120.

Brown, Michael. "Divergent Paths: Early Zionism in Canada and the U.S." *Jew Soc. St.* XLIV, 1982 p. 149-168.

Caplan, N. "From Powerlessness to Power: Zionism in Theory and Practice 1882-1950." *Historical Journal*. 33, 1990, p. 177-108.

Dubnow, Simon. *Jewish History: An Essay with Philosophy of History*. Phila., 1903. DS118 D81

Elam, Yigal. "New look at an old face: Zionism re-examined." *New Middle East* June 1973.

Elboim-Dror, Rachel. "Herzl,s Radical Vision Changed World History" *CJN*, Feb.15, 1996. p.9.

Fackenheim, Emil L. "The Three Pillars of Today's Zionism." *Viewpoints* 10, 7, 1992: 3 & 6.

Gordis, David M. "Zionism, Israel & World Jewry: A Reappraisal." *Judaism* vol. 39, #3, June 1990: 262-275.

Greenstein, Howard. *Turning Point: Zionism and Reform Judaism*. Ann Anbor, 1981. BM 197 G72

Hertzberg, Arthur (ed.) *The Zionist Idea*. N.Y. 1969.
Khouri, T. J. *Arab-Israeli Dilemma* Syracuse 1968.
Klein, A.M. *Zionism, A National Will To Live*, Montreal, 1937.
Kook, Rav. *The Essential Writings of A.I. Kook*. N.Y. 1988. BM45 K646
Margalit, Avishai. "Israel: The Rise of the Ultra Orthodox" *N.Y. Review of Books*. Nov. 9, 1989, p. 38.
Nordau, Max. "On the situation of the Jews throughout the world." - 1897. From *The Jubilee of the First Zionist Congress 1897-1947*. Jerusalem, 1947. DS149A4Z5.
Pinsker, Leon. *"Autoemancipation"* Pamphlet. 1880's DS149 P55 1903 (in German)
Reinharz, Jehuda and Shapira, Anita (Editors). *Essential Papers on Zionism*, New York, 1996, DS149E76.
Rushdie, Salman. "A secular Jew affirms his membership in a culture while being separate from the theology" From text of speech (Dec. 11, 1991 at Columbia University) adapted form as forthcoming essay entitled "One Thousand Days in a Balloon." *N.Y. Times*. Dec. 12: 91, p. B6.
Sacks, Jonathan. "A challenge to Jewish Secularism" *Jewish Spectator* Summer 1990, p. 26-32.
Schwartz (ed.) *The Menorah Treasury*. Philadelphia 1964.
Staniscawski, Howard. *Canadian Zionism, Directions for the 80's*. Montreal, 1980. DS 149 S658

CHAPTER 9

SEPHARDIM IN MONTREAL

Over a dark coffee, he talked about being one of the first French-speaking Jewish men of letters in Montreal, "a French-speaking Jew from Iraq—no one had heard of such a possibility in Montreal in 1954."

There are 27 books listed in the McGill Library system written by Naim Kattan. His style is certainly subjective and draws the reader into the continuous battle between the different groups of Montreal. One of his primary aims is to show, even teach, the people of Quebec that, whatever their culture, there are parallels with other cultures.

He is a proud man who feels that he has accomplished his goal. Many people seem to agree, since he has assembled a number of honours—the Order of Canada, the Order of Quebec, and the Segal Prize For Contribution to Jewish Studies.

For a man dedicated to literature and teaching, another highlight of his life is the inculcation of the passion of learning in his son, Emannuel, who is a Rhodes Scholar.

Sephardim in Montreal
The founding synagogue in Montreal which was dominated by the Sephardim, was the Shearith Israel, now called the Spanish and Portuguese. The population of Sephardim then stagnated until the collapse of the Ottoman Empire in 1914.

Worldwide, the Sephardim had largely accepted their host country's language and characteristics, therefore each community within the Sephardic spectrum had different customs and religious observance.

When the wrath of Arab nationalism, buttressed by Islamic Fundamentalism, forced almost all the Jews out (between 1948 and 1967), there was a huge influx of principally French-speaking Sephardim to Montreal. For example, between 1957 and 1965, 2951 Moroccan, 57 Algerian, and 222 Persian Jews immigrated to Canada through Montreal.[1]

On arrival, the main body of Sephardim came up against the English and/or Yiddish speaking Ashkenazis who headed the firmly entrenched Jewish community. All associations were English-speaking and the Askenazis didn't want to change to accommodate the new arrivals.

Table 18: Montreal's Sephardic Community—1994

Country of Origin	Population	Language	Arrival	District Lived in
Morocco	18,000	1,500 Spanish 16500 French	'60-'70	Chomedey Cote-Vertu Cote-des-Neiges D.D.O.
Iberia	1,500	Span/Port		Downtown
Algeria/Tunisia	400	French	'50-'60	?
Egyptian	1000	Arabic	'20 '40-'60	T.M.R. Outremont
Lebanon	500	Arabic/French	'70-'80	Cote-Vertu
Iran	?	Farsi		Most went to L.A.
Syria	800	Arabic		D.D.O. 150-200 families
Iraq	?	Arabic		?
Turkey	?			?
Greece and Balkans	?			?

meeting with D. Amar, 1994

For the Moroccans it was easier to communicate with fellow French speakers than attaining anything from the English Jewish community—this was the case, even into the 1980's. This is illustrated by the fact that the Federation CJA (new linguistically hybrid French-English name) staff work and publications were only in English well into the 1980's. The Communauté Sépharade du Québec (C.S.Q.) was formed to combat these slights and to keep their French-speaking community informed. In 1996 the C.S.Q. works within the FCJA, all publications are bilingual, and the FCJA staff is almost bilingual. But the C.S.Q. is still wary—a minority within a minority.[2]

Notes

1. Kage, Joseph. "The North African Jewish Immigrant in Montreal." from *Studies & Documents on Immigrants and Integration in Canada* (Montreal, June 1968) (JIAS) Jewish Immigration Aid Services of Canada. FC 1045933 #11. p.2.
2. Shahar, Charles. "A Survey of Jewish Life in Montreal." *Fed J.C.S. of Montreal.* Dec. 1996. p.28-9.

References

Alboim, Naomi et al. "Moroccan Jews in Montreal." *Strobe* 4 Fall 1970: 27-30.

Amber P., & Lipper I. "Toward an understanding of Moroccan Jewish family life." *U. of McGill Social Work*, 1968 Thesis. AS47m 39 1968 A43

Batshaw, H. & Lowe, B. *The Integration of Moroccan Jewish Immigrants in Montreal (1964-70)* AS 42 M33 1971 B37. M.A. Thesis, McGill U.

Berdugo - Cohen, Marie, Y. Cohen, & Joseph Levy. *Juif Moroccan à Montréal.* 1987. FC 2947.9 J4 B47.

Berman, Gerald, Nahmiash, D & Osmer C. *A Profile of Moroccan Jewish Immigrants in Montreal 1957-1967.* MA Thesis 1970 AS 42 M33 1970 B47.

Dahan, Simon & Chokron, Michel. "Rapport de l'Enquête sur la population sépharde de l'agglomération montréalaise—1988". Montreal CSQ 1989. 33 pages.

Dobrinsky, H. *A Treasury of Sephardic Laws & Customs*. N.Y., 1986. BM 700 D56.
Elazar, Daniel. *The Other Jews: The Sephardim Today*. N.Y. 1989. DS 134 E4
Elbaz, André. "A new immigration to Canada: North African Jews in Montreal". *J. of Can. St.* vol. 3, Feb. 1968. F5000 J6
Elbaz, Mikhael. "D'immigrants à Ethniques" (1989) from Lesry & Tapia 1989, p. 81-101.
Filion, E.G. "La communauté sépharade de Montréal". Dept. of Anthro. Quebec, U. of Laval 1978.
Fuerstenbers, Adam. "The Sephardim of Toronto: a minority with a minority". *Polyphony* 6 1 (print - the 1984) 159-161.
Kattan, Naim. *Les juifs et la communauté français*. Montréal 1965. FC 106 J5 J85.
_____. *Farewell, Babylon*. Montreal, 1976. PS 8571 A88 A73
Kage, Joseph. "The North African Jewish Immigrant in Montreal." from *Studies & Documents on Immigrants and Integration in Canada* (Montreal, June 1968) (JIAS) Jewish Immigration Aid Services of Canada. FC 1045933 #11. 13 pages.
Hirchberg, J.J. *Secular & Parochial Education of Ashkenzi & Sephardic Jewish Children in Montreal* 1988, Ph.D. Thesis. Education AS42 M3 1989 H54
Laskier, Michael M. "A note on Present-day Sephardim and Oriental Jewry." *Jewish Journal of Sociology* 35, 2; Dec. '93: 135-140.
Lasry, J.C. & Tapia C. *Les Juifs de Maghreb—diaspora contemporaires*. Montreal, 1989. DS 134 J85.
Lasry, Jean Claude. "Sephardim & Askenazim in Montreal" *Contemporary Jewry* 1983, 6, 2: 26-33. at S.G.W.U.
Lasry, Jean Claude. "A francophone diaspora in Quebec" p. 221-240. from *The Canadian Jewish Mosaic*. Weinfeld, Saffir, & Cotler. Toronto, 1981. FC 106J5C28.
Lasry, Jean Claude, "Essor et tradition: La communauté jeune nord-Afrique au Québec". p. 19-53.
Lesser, Julie. "Sephardic community at once integrated, distinct" .Montreal Gazette, June 11, 1996 p. B5 b.
Levy, J. and Cohen, Yoland "Moroccan Jews and their Adaptation to Montreal Life." *Reviewing Our Ways*. Robinson/Butovsky, p. 95-118.
Levy, Joseph, & Ouaknire, Leon. (from Lasry & Tapia) "Institutions communautaires: des juifs marocain à Montréal" p. 57-75.
Moldofsky, Naomi. *The Economic Adjustment of North African Jewish Immigrants in Montreal*. McG. Doctorate 1968. F5417 M6 1968.
Papo, Joseph M. *Sephardim in 20th century North America*. San Jose, 1987. E 184 J5 P29

Schmelz, V.O. et al. "Ethnic differences among Israel: Jews: A new look". *AJYB*, 1990. E 184 J5 A6

Shaha, Charles. "A Survey of Jewish Life in Montreal." *Fed J.C.S. of Montreal.* Dec. 1996.

Stern, Malcolm H. "Portuguese Sephardim in the Americas." *American Jewish Archives*. Spring Summer 1992, p. 141-178, Montreal, p. 169-70.

Stillman, Norman A. *The Jews of Arab Lands in Modern Times*. Phila. 1991. DS 135 A68 575.

Torczyner, "Sephardim" p. 69-72 in McGill Consortium (et al.) publication.

Waller, H. "Canada" *AJYB* 1991 p. 235.

Weinfeld, Morton & Lasry, J.G. "Sephardim & Ashkenazim in Montreal" *Contemporary Jewry* 6, 2: 83.

Zimmers, Rabbi H.J. *Ashkenazim & Sephardim* London, 1958. BM 182 Z5 1969.

Canadian Jewish News, "Condition of Sephardic Jewry, focus of G.A. Panel Discussion". Jan. 13, 1994, p. 7.

_____, "CSQ helps to improve Sephardic quality of life" Nov. 14, 1991, p. 13.

_____, "Le CSQ nous présente un magnifique Album sépharade" October 6, 1994, p. 2.

_____, "Study Looks at Sephardim Community." Oct. 5, 1995, p. 12.

CHAPTER 10

ASHKENAZIM IN MONTREAL

Orthodoxy

There are three Jewish groups in Montreal that can be classified as Orthodox—the Orthodox, the Orthodox Hasidim, and the Neo-Orthodox.

Orthodox Jews are observant of the Torah, restrictive in their mode of dress, and go to parochial schools. They are not Hasidic, and they live predominately in the Darlington-Wilderton-de Viny district. They number approximately 400 families.

Orthodox Hasidism has 10 courts in Montreal, basically in four areas: Park Avenue, Outremont, Snowdon and Boisbriand. They all maintain their own world. The young children look like their parents: the girls wear long multi-coloured dresses with head coverings, and the boys wear somber jackets and trousers. Their parents are easily distinguishable since the men wear all black, and have shtrymlaches (fur-trimmed wide-brimmed hats) flowing beards and payis (side curls), while the women are be-wigged (a married woman shaves her head to avoid tempting men) with head scarf and ankle-length dresses. By having their own schools and having no television, the children are restricted from an open education. The average number of children in each family is five, well above the average of two in other Ashkenazi homes.

Table 19: Orthodox Hasidism in Greater Montreal

Court Name	# of Families
Lubavitch	350
Satmar	120
Belz	160
Skver	60
Vishnitz	60
Muncacz	25
Pupa	20
Klausenberg	15
Santzer	10
Tash (Boisbriand)	160
Total	**980**

Ms.C. Polter

Neo-Orthodox is a nebulous term—it could be called Modern Orthodox. The Neo-Orthodox live in a modern world, maybe with secular education, certainly with television, and are less observant in their eating practices; and may live away from their synagogue, but they still believe in the tenets of Orthodoxy. The numbers and the whereabouts of the Neo-Orthodox are impossible to pin down. The locations of their Orthodox synagogues provide only a very rough indicator of their living habits.

Non-Orthodoxy

Again the main groups are:
   A. Conservatism
   B. Reconstructionism
   C. Reform

Real difficulties in isolating their numbers and geographic areas occur. One can count the synagogues, and estimate or ask for the number of families that are members, but still come up with no real answer. Studies by Cohen, Torczyner, Shahar and older studies of Rosenberg indicate low attendance at the synagogues for these groups.

Secular

Added to the problems of determining the numbers and location of the observant Jew is the growing number of secular Jews. They can hold the tenets of Orthodoxy, be Conservative, Reconstructionist, Reform, purely Zionist, atheist, or of smaller sects (such as the Jews for Jesus), but do not join a synagogue,m but often attending only for the High Holidays.

Special Groups

Within the Orthodox, Non-Orthodox, and Secular groups, there are large associations of Holocaust survivors. Also, the newly arrived Russians, with sparse religious knowledge of Judaism, are an increasingly conspicuous group.

Table 20: Simplified schematic view of Judaism*

Secular	Reform	Reconstructionists	Conservatives	Orthodox	Ultra-O.
|	|		|	|	|
many guises	•Classic		•liberal •traditionalist	•Neo- •more observant to the Torah	Hasidim

* *Zionists can be in any sect— except Hasidic Satmars*

Table 21: Religious Parallels

Judaism				
Secular	.... Reform	.... Conservative	. Orthodox	..... Ultra Orthodox

Christianity
Secular .... Baptist .... Anglican .... Roman. .... Fundamentalist
• Chruch • Low   Catholic   • Amish
of God • High   • "Born Again"

Islam
Secular .... Conservative .... Fundamentalist
different degrees
due to level of emancipation

References

Barth, F. *Ethnic Groups and Boundaries: The Social Organization of Cultural Differences* Boston 1969. GN320E77

Chartrand, Luc. "Juifs des pays" (TASH) *Actualité* 16 #70 (15 dec. 91), p. 52-60. AP21 A33X.

Gutwirth, Jacques. "The structure of a Hassidic Community in Montreal." *Jew J. of Soc.* 141 (June 1972) 43-62. DS101 J4657

Lazarus, David. "Local Eruv may be revived." *C.J. News.* Jan 19, 1996, p. 6.

Polter, Carol. Interview, March 2, 1994.

Regenstreif, Michael. *Gazette* May 21, 1992 on Shaffir and Hasidic sects.

Robinson, Ira & Butovsky, M. *Renewing Our Days.* Montreal Jews in the 20th Century. Montreal, 1995.

Shaffir, William "Separate from the Mainstream in Canada: The Hasidic Community of Tash" *Jew J. of Sociology* XXIX: 1: Jan. 1987: 19-35. McL DS 101 J4657

Shaffir, William. "Hasidic Jews & Quebec Politics". *Jew J. of Sociology* XXV: #2 Dec. 83, p. 105-118.

Shaffir, William. "Becoming an Orthodox Chassidic Jew: The Socialization of Newcomers to a Religious Community". *Can Ethnic Studies* Vol. VI, 1978, p. 295-309.

Shaffir, William. "Jewish Messianism Lubavitch-Style: An Interim Report." *Jew J. of Sociology*, v. 135, #2 Dec. 1993.

Zylberberg, Jacques et al. "De la mystique au pouvoir: étatisation et dépolitisation des hassidim Montréalais". *Conférence Internationale de Sociologie des Religions: ACTES* 18 (1985) 221-26.

PART III

PROBLEMS

CHAPTER 11

JEWISH WOMEN AND EQUALITY

I first heard of Norma Joseph when I attended a meeting at the Jewish Public Library where she gave a spirited talk on women's rights in marriage and divorce. Discussions on the Get (a Jewish marriage contract) and the abolition of its obligatory clauses in Canada were eye openers to me; I didn't realize that the husband had control of the divorce and therefore the marriage.

Two years later, I had an intense interview with her in her office.

The solitary chair in front of a desk in front of Professor Norma Joseph looked very lonely. I was asked in for my interview and motioned to sit. A quandry—do I shake hands? If Prof. Joseph is highly Orthodox, she doesn't want to touch me. Well, I did, and then sat down. And she was sitting down too, behind her huge desk, far away.

I had sent her a few pages of information so I asked the first question: "Taking into account the patriarchal assumptions of the halakah, what is the woman's place in the Jewish life of Montreal?" She rolled her eyes and held her head in her hands. "Let's have a simple question," she replied.

We discussed marriage, bat mitzvah, divorce and the Get, equality in the workplace, outmarriage and the great advances that women have made in education and religious matters. We covered the waterfront, but only superficially until I mentioned my concept of dualism (supporting Canada and

Israel). That lit a fuse, but it fizzled when the phone rang. When we returned to the interview, it was really finished. I tried to rekindle the discussion, but minds were elsewhere and I left. 52 minutes in that chair was enough.

Jewish Women

"Blessed are you, Lord our G-d, King of the Universe who has not made me a woman"—with this prayer the Orthodox men begin each day.[1] This is another example of the pervasive theme of male dominance.

Historically in religious practice, woman's "place" is evident. Today the dominance of men has somewhat lessened in the practice of religion.

Table 22: Dominance of Gender—major religions

	Center	(Leader) Head	Homeland	Domination
Islam	to Mecca in one's life time	1 God no dominant since last Caliph	None	Male
Roman Catholic	Highly institutional Rome	1 God Pope infallibility	None	Male
Protestant	fractured	1 God None	None	mostly male
Judaism	Jerusalem lightly mystical	1 God None	Israel	Male
Hinduism	highly mystical	many gods	None	male and castes
Buddhism	fractured	1 God None	None	Male

The degree of women's rights is a gauge for the amount of openness and respect towards women in one's society.

In Judaism, there is a wide diversity of the woman's role in religion. In the Ultra-orthodox and most other Orthodox sects, the women are segregated from men in public prayer. In fact, some pray in separate rooms or balconies. To answer critics, the traditionalists fall back on Jewish Law divined by the Torah, and quote Leviticus to block the social, religious progress of women's rights given in Reform and some Conservative Synagogues, where the women sit and even sing in pews with their male companions.

I recently went to a bar mitzpah at the Chevra Kadisha-B'Nai Jacob synagogue. All the men sat on the middle pews, many with prayer shawls, while the women in all their finery and wonderful hats, sat on the side pews beside the walls of the synagogue.

The film "Half the Kingdom—Seven Jewish Feminists" (1985) describes the trauma of being a woman in a man's society. For the first time in Jewish history, women are making their place in Jewish society—in a drive for equality. Single women, divorcees, widows, and older women are trying to gain more rights and compassion in Jewish society. If the established tenets of Judaism do not change with this new thrust, then it jeopardizes its own survival. The tendency is to move to secularism, which causes an increase in outmarriage. Reading Nora Gold's work, I was amazed by the wide array of problems that Jewish women have in today's world, especially in the area of what she calls the "allure of the non-Jewish world".[2]

One of the problems in the male dominated religion is when a marriage breaks up. Divorce—Jewish religious divorce—the Get—must be authorized by the male in Orthodoxy. A married woman is an agunah —Hebrew for chained woman. The plight of agunot—women whose husbands have refused granting the Get—was abolished in

Canada, in 1990, by a new divorce law. Professor Norma Joseph helped the formation of this law in Canada. Women now are helped by this law when the problem of being separated from or deserted by men occurs because couples must "remove all barriers" when divorcing, and the law allows for penalties if the male (or the female) refuses.

Another problem is abortion—"I call heaven and earth to record this day against you, that I have set before your life and death, blessing and cursing: therefore choose life that both thou and thy seed may live..." (Deuteronomy 30:19). Based on this passage, the Orthodox community generally opposes non-therapeutic abortion; the Conservative and Reform groups generally support elective abortion. Secular Jews see the issue as not just about choice but about the protection of human rights.

Notes
1. *Prayer Book for Sabbath & Festivals Hebrew.* Pub.Co. N.Y. 1964. p.86
2. Gold, Nora. "Antisemitism and Sexism in the Experience of Canadian Women" (unpublished paper) McMaster University, 1996, very good bibliography.

References
Aaron, Scott. "The choice in 'choose life'" in *Commonweal*, Feb. 28, 1992. p. 15-18.
Arnold, Janice. in *C.J.N.* March 18, 1993; Feb. 17,1994; March 3, 1994; Sept. 22, 1994.
Benjamin, Marina. "Judaism's second-class citizens." *Manchester Guardian* July 11, 1993, p. 23.
Canfor, Aviva. *Jewish Women /Jewish Men : The Legacy of Patriarchy in Jewish Life* San Francisco, 1995.
Fishbane, Simcha. "A Female Rite of Passage in a Montreal Modern Orthodox Synagogue: The Bat Mitzvah Ceremony." p. 119-131, from *Renewing our Days* Robinson/Butovsky.
Gold, Nora. "Antisemitism and Sexism in the Experience of Canadian Women" (unpublished paper) McMaster University, 1996, very good bibliography.

Gornick, Vivian. "Twice an outsider: On being Jewish and a woman" *Tikkun* 4 #2, p. 29-31, & 123-5.

Haberman, Clyde. "Rabbis Decide Some Israelis Cannot Marry." *N.Y. Times* Dec. 23, 1994, P. A.11

Hertz, Deborah. "Jewish women in Europe 1750-1932: A Bibliography Guide." *Jewish History*, 7, 2, 1993 p. 127-153.

Hyman, Paula E. "Ezrat Nashim and the Emergence of New Jewish Feminism," p. 284-295 in *The Americanization of the Jews*. R.M. Seltzer & N.J. Cohen (editors) N.Y. 1995. E 184 J5 A618

Joseph, Norma B. "The Feminist Challenge to Judaism: Critique and Transformation." M. Joy & Ek. Neumaier—Dargay (ed) *Gender, Genre and Religion* Waterloo, 1995. BL 458 G45.

Kraemer, David. "Jewish Ethics and Abortion" *Tikkun* 8 #1, p. 55-58 & 77-79.

Lazarus, David. "Yeshivah Caters to Women." *C.J.N.* Feb. 1: 96, p. 8.

Magnus, Shulamit "... "Out of the Ghetto":Integrating the study of Jewish women into the study of 'The Jews'" (a reconstructionist) *Judaism* vol. 39:1 winter 1990: 28-36.

Plaskov, Judith. "The year of the Agunah" *Tikkun* 8 #5, p. 52-3 & 86-7.

Riskin, Shlomo, *Women and Jewish Divorce*. Hoboken, 1989.

Silverman, Eliane. "Jewish Women Talking About Jewish Women (On Activism and "At Home") "A Heritage in Transition" - Jewish Studies in Canada - Conference June 10,1996, Concordia University.

Sullivan, Renald "Refusing to agree to a religious divorce proves costly" in *N.Y. Times* Oct. 5, 1994, p. B3.

Torczyner, Jim, & Brotman, Shari. "Jewish Continuity in Canada" *Viewpoints* 22 #2, 1994, p. 4.

Torczyner, J.M. "Jewish Women & Inequality in the Labour Force" McGill Consortium for Ethnicity and Strategic Social Planning Report or Montreal Jews 1994, p. 162-3.

Warwick, Liz. "A life of pushing limits" *Gazette* Aug. 14, 1995, p. C1.

Weissman, Deborah. "The Jewish woman: Traditions and Transitions" in *Studies in Contemporary Jewry* #5 1989: 279-288.

Zerker, Sally. "How I gave up the Mechitzah for Good" *Viewpoints* XXI, #4 1993: 7-8.

Prayer Book for Sabbath & Festivals Hebrew. Pub.Co. N.Y. 1964

CHAPTER 12

FERTILITY

"The rate of fertility has fallen so low in Canada that the replacement of the present generation is no longer assumed".[1] In discussing the demography of Jewish Diaspora, Schmelz delineated the main streams of Judaism and their low fertility compared to other ethnic groups. He also depicted other factors that result in lower fertility, such as changes in matrimonial mores and later marriage and family formation.

Table 23: Fertility Analysis—AJYB 1981

	Fertility	Longevity
Ashkenazi	Low	High
Hasidic	High	High
Sephardic		
Mediterranean countries	High	High
North America	Low	High
Oriental (Middle East)	High	High

High longevity results in a lower percentage of the women population at child-bearing age. Other factors—(a) with greater mobility of families there are fewer children, (b) increase of out-marriage and loss of ties to Jewish community, (c) marginal religious Jews—secular Jews losing their identity—i.e. assimilating, and (d) low fertility becomes a characteristic of Jews when they become more emancipated.[2]

This depressed rate of fertility in Montreal can be also affected by (1) Russian Jews' minority group status, (2) urbanization, (3) higher education levels, or (4) by both spouses being involved in the labour force. With many adults of child bearing age leaving Montreal since 1976, there is a dramatic change in overall fertility levels, which is compounded by the fact that there have been decreased rates of nuptiality.

Notes
1. Romaninc, A. *Fertility in Canada: Baby Boom to Baby-Bust* HB939-R65 Stats. Can. Ottawa, 1984 (91-524E). In French HB939-R66.
2. Ritterband, (Ed) *Modern Jewish Fertility*, Leider, Netherlands, 1981 DS143M6. p.383.

References
Balakishnan, T.R. et al. *Family & Childbearing in Canada*. Toronto 1993. HB 939 B35

Chamie, J. *Religion & Fertility* Cambridge, England, 1981. HQ 663.9 C47.

Caldwell, Gary. *Les déterminants de l'évolution récente de la fécondité au Québec*. Quebec 1992. HB 940 Q3C35

Goldstein, Sidney. "Jewish Fertility in Contemporary America" p. 160-208 from *Modern Jewish Fertility*. Ritterband

Halli, S. *Ethnic Demography: Canadian Immigrant, Racial and Cultural Variations*. Ottawa, 1990.

Ritterband, Paul. "Modern Times and Jewish Assimilation," p. 377-394 in *Americanization of the Jews*. Seltzer and Cohen.

Ritterband, (Ed) *Modern Jewish Fertility*, Leider, Netherlands, 1981 DS143M6

Romaninc, A. *Fertility in Canada: Baby Boom to Baby-Bust* HB939-R65 Stats. Can. Ottawa, 1984 (91-524E). In French HB939-R66.

Rose, Ben. "There is more decline in Jewish numbers from low birth rates than from intermarriage". Quoting S. Cohen. C.J.N. May 28, 92.

Schmelz, V.O. "Jewish Survival: The Demographic Factors." *AJYB* 1981, p. 68-108.

Seltzer Robert M. and Steven M. Cohen. *The Americanization of the Jews* N.Y. 1995 E184J5A618.

Weeks, John R. *Population* (4th ed.) Belmont, Ca. 1989. HB871.W43

CHAPTER 13

OUTMARRIAGE

There is parental disapproval, peer pressure, and fear of the unknown to deal with when a Jew falls in love with one of the goyim. (There is also a shock when an Ultra-Orthodox Jew marries a Reform Jew). But the problem of an out-marriage is the loss of the Jewish faith in the partners if there is no conversion, and the subsequent loss to Judaism of the couple's children. The term out-marriage is more specific than mixed marriage or intermarriage as it specifically is the marriage between different religions not just sects.

Table 24: Outmarriage Selected Areas (1991)

U.S.A.	28%
Canada	13%
Vancouver	25%
Montreal	7%

Friesel, and Torczyner

Many dilemmas arise in the community. The couple wants to get married, but where? In Montreal, no Conservatives and only one Reform Rabbi will perform the marriage if there is conversion, while no traditionalist will do so under any conditions (it is against Jewish law). If a Rabbi doesn't perform the wedding, the couple will in all probability leave the Jewish community.

Jewish Law recognizes the children of a Jewish mother as

being Jewish. What about the Jewish father and his outmarriage children? Many Rabbis reject out-marriage children. Is it time for the Rabbis to re-examine their approach to intermarriage?[1] The community should embrace these couples instead of showing its ignorance and lack of understanding.[2] The FCJA's Outreach to the Intermarried Committee is contested by Orthodox rabbis who say that bringing interfaith families into the community could undermine the credibility of Jewish tradition.[3] Conversion to Judaism by a spouse is an exhausting process due to the new and complex wordings and rituals of Judaism (which are easier to learn at an earlier stage in life). This deters some.

The second marriage of spouses has an even higher outmarriage frequency. The males remarry more often, and have a higher out-marriage percentage than the females.

With the females outnumbering the males (101 to 100 percentile), males out-marrying females 60% to 40% for the first out-marriage, and the males remarrying 60% to the females' 40%, spinsters, divorcees, and those separated to look for husbands outside Judaism.[4]

Many Jewish organizations look to control the urge towards intermarriage, such as the Canadian Commission on Jewish Identity and Continuity. Others condemn the attempt of the commission. For example, the ultra-orthodox Jews could never go along with the idea of any "consensus" that they couldn't veto.

One finds that the Canadian Jew's outlook is somewhat more traditional than his U.S. counterpart, but the infusion of American views is insidious. There is great interplay and two way migration between the two countries' Jewish communities. In the U.S.A., Jews have a larger proportion of Reform and secular Jews than in Canada, so their intermarriage problem is more acute.

Another factor is that the Jews in any community must attain a certain level of population making it possible to marry

Graphic 1: Will Your Grandchild be Jewish?

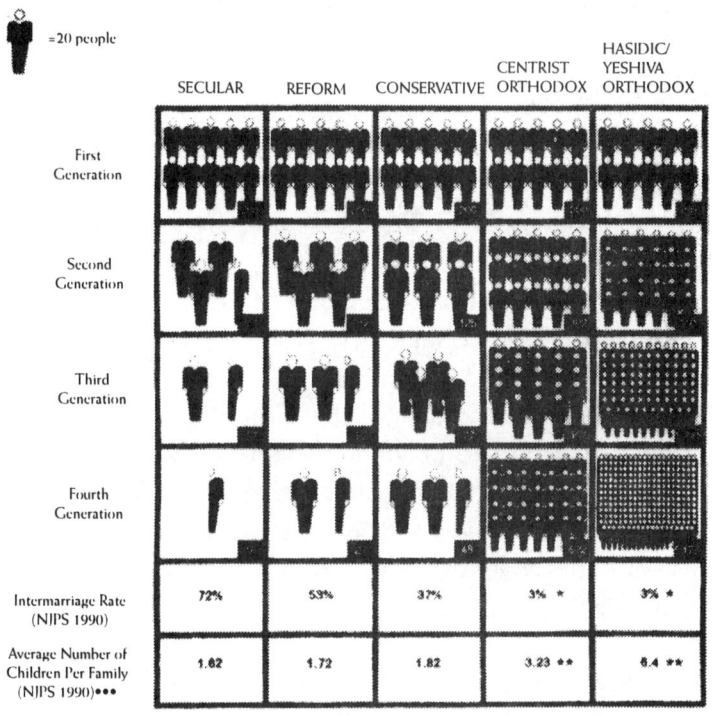

- No sufficient data to distinguish between "Centrist Orthodox" and "Hasidic-Yeshiva Orthodox" for purposes of intermarriage rates.
- Although there is no clear definition of "Centrist Orthodox" or "Hasidic" Yeshiva "Orthodox" the main distinguishing factor relates to attitudes regarding formal secular studies and family size.
- •Gordon and Horowitz Independant Survey (1994)
- ••Based on current intermarriage rates and the average number of children per family, the chnaces of young contempory Jews having Jewish grandchildren and great-grandchildren, with the exception of the Orthodox, are increasingly remote.

Dershowitz, Alan M. *The Vanishing American Jew* Boston 1997, p.26.

within their own community and escape further attrition through randomization.

The Orthodox way of life, ardent about observing Jewish law, almost precludes intermarriage. When the more liberal movement "abandoned the primacy of religion and law as pillars of Jewish individual and communal life, they failed to substitute a sufficiently compelling and intensive attachment to Judaism to ensure Jewish survival".[5]

Alan Dershowitz, in his latest book *The Vanished American Jew*, writes,

How to Make Sure Your Child Marries a Jew
I tell my audience that there is, of course, one near-certain way to prevent intermarriage. Suddenly everyone in the audience pays rapt attention. Some even take out notepads and begin to wriete, as I describe the preventative steps that can be taken. Here they are—the seven-step program to guarantee that yuor children and grandchildren will marry a Jewish spouse:

1. Move to a totally Orthodox Jewish shtetl like New Square in Rockland Couty, New York.
2. Do not teach your children any English. Teach them only Yiddish and Hebrew.
3. Prohibit all access to television, radio, movies, nespapers, computers, and any other gateways to the outside world.
4. Teach the boys a tradein which only other Orthodox Jews work, such as diamond cutting. Do not teach the girls a trade, and do not let them work outside the home.
5. Do not allow your children to go to school with non-Jews, and certainly not to college.
6. Teach them to regard all gentilles—and non-Orthodox Jews—with suspicion, if not contempt.

7. Arrange their marriage and have them marry by the time they are seventeen....this is the Hasidic way of life.

Notes

1. Sobel, Miriam. "Report comments on intermarriage rights" *C.J.N.* Aug. 13, 1992 p. 2.
2. Schoenfeld, Stuart. "Assimilation, Intermarriage, Jewish Identity" *Viewpoints.* May 5, 1988, p. 7.
3. Arnold, Janice. "Outreach Plan Prompts Skepticism Among Orthodox" *C J News,* Dec. 21, 1995, p. 3.
4. Medding, Peter et al. "Jewish Identity in Conversionary and Mixed Marriages" *American Jewish Year Book 1992* p. 3-43.
5. Gordis, Daniel. "Jewish Love, Jewish Law: Can Liberal Judaism Weather the Intermarriage Crisis?" *Jewish Spectator* Winter 1991-2, p. 6.

References

Arnold, Janice. "Outreach Plan Prompts Skepticism Among Orthodox" *C J News,* Dec. 21, 1995, p. 3.
Della Pergola, S., & Schmelz, V.O. "Demographic Transformation of American Jewry: Marriage—Mixed Marriage in the 80's." *Studies in Contemporary Jewry.* 5: 89, p. 169-200.
Friesel, Evyatar. *Atlas of Modern Jewish History* N.Y. 1990, p.135.
Goldstein, Jay, & Segall, Alexander. "Ethnic Intermarriage & Ethnic Identity." *Can. Ethnic St.* 17: 60-90.
Dershowitz, Alan M. *The Vanishing American Jew* Boston 1997, p.26 and 171.
Goldstein, Sidney. "Perspective from demography" in *American Jews—* Sklare, p. 74-80.
Gordis, Daniel. "Jewish Love, Jewish Law: Can Liberal Judaism Weather the Intermarriage Crisis?" *Jewish Spectator* Winter 1991-2, p. 6-11.
Lambert, R.D., & Curtis D.E. "Québécois & English Canadian opposition to racial and religious intermarriage, 1963-1983" *Canadian Ethnic Studies,* 16, 2, 1984: 30-40.
Lasry, J.-C., Bloomfield, Shachter, E. "Jewish Intermarriage in Montreal 1962-1971" *Jewish Social Studies* 37 #3 1975, p. 267-78.
Lipstadt, Deborah. "The Ties That No Longer Bind" *Jewish Spectator* 1991, p. 62-63.
Mayer, Egon. *Intermarriage & the Jewish Future.* N.Y. 1979. HQ 1031 m 378

Medding, Peter et al. "Jewish Identity in Conversionary and Mixed Marriages" *American Jewish Year Book 1992* p. 3-43.
Renbaum, Dafna. "Diminishing Returns" *Kolenunab*, Summer 1992 p.36-37.
Ritterband, Paul. "Modern Times and Jewish Assimilation" in *Americanization of the Jews*, p. 383.
Schoenberg, Eilliot S. (Rabbi) "Intermarriage and Conservative Judaism: An Approach for the 1990's" *Conservative Judaism* vol. 43(1) Fall 1990: 12-24.
Schoenfeld, Stuart. "Assimilation, Intermarriage, Jewish Identity" *Viewpoints*. May 5, 1988, p. 7.
Singer, David. "Living with Intermarriage" in *American Jews* -Sklare. p. 395-412.
Sklare, Marshall. *Observing American's Jews*. in it a ground breaking article originally published in 1964 "Intermarriage and the Jewish Future" p. 235-247.
_____. (editor) *American Jews—A Reader*. N.Y. 1983.
Sobel, Miriam. "Report comments on intermarriage rights" *C.J.N.* Aug. 13, 1992 p. 2.
Solarchik, Chaya. *Canada/Israel Jewish Marriages*. Rare book Thesis Collection. AS 42 M3 1982 S684.
Tobin, Gary A. "Structural Change, Jewish Identity & Interfaith Marriages of American Jews" *Conservative Judaism* vol. 43(1) Fall 1990: 3-11.
Torczyer, Jim. "Intermarriage" McGill Consortium (et al.) p. 118-20.
Weinfeld, M. "Intermarriage: Agony and Adaptation" in *Canadian Jewish Mosaic*. Toronto, 1981. p. 365-382. FC 106 J5 C28.
C.J.N. "Agudath Israel will not join commission on intermarriage" March 10, 1994, p. 12.

CHAPTER 14

THE AGING AND THE POOR

Aging

In Canada in 1941, the average age was 28.4 years; in 1981 it was 32.6; and in 1991 it was 34.5—Canadians are getting older.

Correspondingly, in 1941, Jews were a young average of 27.4; in 1981, they were 34.6; and in 1991, they were 38.0. The average age of Jews is increasing faster than the average age of Canadians.

In Quebec, the Jews averaged 31.2 years in 1941; 39.9 in 1981; and 41.6 in 1991.

These statistics highlight the problem of aging in the Montreal Jewish Community.

Table 25: Jewish Age Groups in Montreal

	1941	1961	1971	1981	1991
Under 15	13124	27994	22420	17240	17950
%	21	27	20	17	18
15-24	11580	12809	19955	14385	11705
%	18	12	18	14	12
25-44	23365	27661	25420	26615	24775
%	37	26	23	26	26
44-64	17645	27925	31575	24435	20130
%	28	27	28	24	21
Over 65	2820	8375	13525	19525	22150
%	4	8	12	19	23
Total	63475	104727	110885	102355	96710

Statistics Canada

In 1941, 4.4% of the Community was over 65. This increased to 22.8% in 1991. In Toronto, in 1941, 4.6% of the community was over 65, which increased to 14.7 in 1991. Another relevant figure is the comparison between those under 15 and those over 65 in Montreal.

Table 26: Percentage of Selected Jewish Age Groups in Montreal

	15 under %	65 over %
1941	20.7	4.4
1961	26.7	8.0
1971	20.2	12.2
1981	16.8	19.1
1991	17.9	22.9

Statistics Canada

The 1981 figure was the statistical 'watershed' for the Montreal Jewish Community's population, as the percentage of its people being over 65 exceeded the percentage of with children under 15. The proportions continue to show the increase in the aging population.

"It helps to be Jewish because there's a kind of built-in defense, genetically, against suffering and pain and misfortune. So the fact I am Jewish has been certainly a very great help in my being able to deal with old age."[1]

Mr. C. Shahar, examining the 1986 census tracts, broke down the population of the Jewish Community into Ashkenazim and Sephardim in districts closely resembling the 18 previous areas in the chapter on Montreal.

Table 27: Sephardic population by district and age—1986 (Map 4)

District	0-14	15-24	25-44	45-64	65+	Total Pop.
Chomedey	325	240	460	345	45	1435
Cote-des-Neiges	500	380	715	665	520	2785
Cote St-Luc	565	395	930	530	315	2760
Hampstead	230	125	340	210	75	980
Mont-Royal	100	130	260	275	70	840
NDG & Mtl-West	145	100	190	160	135	770
Outremont	90	80	145	60	45	430
Park/Centre Ville	85	80	245	110	105	655
Ville St-Laurent	445	305	695	630	220	2305
Snowdon	215	140	300	180	155	1000
West Island	320	200	485	260	55	1340
Westmount	110	70	215	140	135	670
Rest of Mtl.	265	300	530	185	70	1385
Total Mtl. CMA	3435	2605	5540	3800	1985	17360

C. Shahar

Table 28: Ashkenazi population by district and age—1986 (Map 4)

District	0-14	15-24	25-44	45-64	65+	Total Pop.
Chomedey	910	1295	1380	1710	400	5795
Cote-des-Neiges	805	425	955	1315	2995	6395
Cote St-Luc	2195	2110	3555	4635	5110	17605
Hampstead	1010	1100	1555	1450	1580	6700
Mont-Royal	440	355	645	495	310	2265
NDG & Mtl-West	905	650	1745	935	1360	5615
Outremont	1005	310	635	265	320	2550
Park/Centre Ville	425	295	1235	655	850	3486
Ville St-Laurent	705	760	1315	1540	1090	5415
Snowdon	410	235	670	720	1820	3870
West Island	2736	915	2910	555	125	7255
Westmount	960	925	1765	1535	1315	6585
Rest of Mtl.	1130	395	1245	510	260	3245
Total Mtl. CMA	13660	9845	19610	16390	17550	77060

C. Shahar

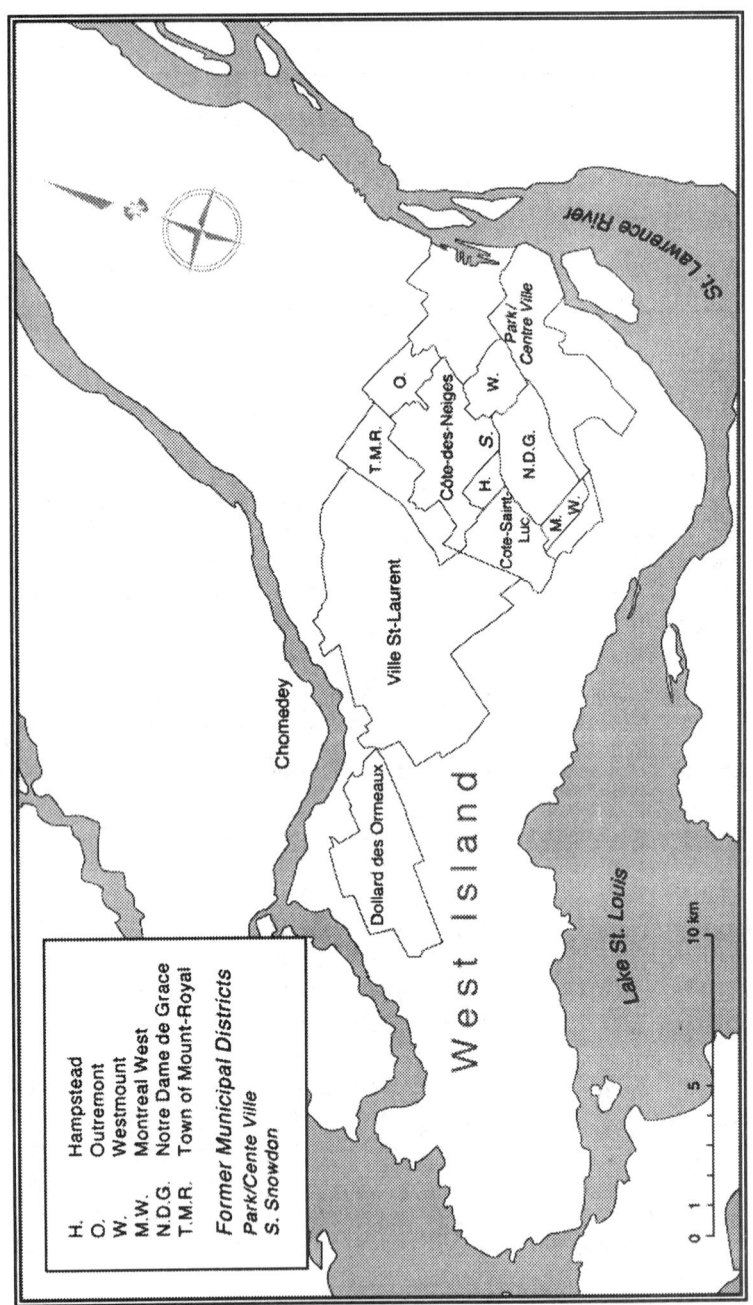

Map 4: Sephardic and Ashkenazi populations by district and age

The average age of the Ashkenazi Community is 40.8 and that of the Sephardim is 35.7. The over 65 years of age portion of the statistics is very important as it highlights the further problems of care for the elderly.

Table 29: Evolution in the Percentage of People aged 65 and over, by Ethnic Group, Quebec 1931-1981.

Ethnic Group	1931	1941	1951	1961	1971	1981	1991
Ukrainian	0.3	1.3	3.4	5.8	10.9	19.9	*
Jewish	2.5	4.7	6.4	8.0	12.0	18.	*
Polish	0.8	2.0	3.5	4.8	9.2	17.1	*
British	6.2	8.0	9.6	9.7	10.1	13.1	*
German	4.3	5.6	6.7	4.0	6.2	10.4	*
Italian	2.0	3.0	5.2	3.4	4.2	7.8	*
French	4.7	4.9	5.2	5.4	6.4	7.7	*
All of Quebec	4.8	5.3	5.7	5.8	6.9	8.3	10.4
Roman Catholic							10.3
Protestant							13.4
Jewish							22.9

Statistics Canada, * 1991 unavailable

Living to an older age than in the past produces a change in mortality rates. The table #30 exhibit the dramatic changes in aging in Canada and Quebec.

Table 30: Average Age of Mortality

Year	Canada	Quebec	diff.
1931	62.0	57.0	-5.0
1941	64.5	61.7	-2.8
1951	68.5	66.6	-1.9
1961	71.3	70.5	-0.8
1976	73.8	73.2	-0.6

Bourbeau & Légaré

Another study charts the life expectancy in certain districts in Montreal, factoring in the districts' economic conditions.

Table 31: Life Expectancy of Selected Areas—Montreal, 1976

NDG 75.6	Higher Level of
Côte-des-Neiges 75.4	Household Income
Ahuntsic 73.4	
Villeray 72.4	
Plat. Mt. Royal 70.8	
Verdun 69.7	Lower Level of
St. Henri area 68.5	Household Income

Wilkins

Other ethnic groups of Montreal have much smaller aging populations.

Table 32: Ages of Three Religious Groups

	Canada			Montreal		
	Jews	E.Ortho.	Islam	Jews	E.Ortho	Islam
Total	318000	387000	253000	96700	88300	41200
-15	62000	61000	71000	17900	15000	11800
15-29	37000	59000	40000	11700	15100	5900
24-44	97000	115000	99000	24800	25200	18400
45-64	63000	98000	35000	20000	21800	4300
+65	59000	53000	8000	22100	8200	700
+65 by %	14.6%	13.7%	3.2%	22.8%	9.3%	2.0%

Statistics Canada

Being single, isolated, or disabled hampers the life of the aged. A significant number of aged over 75 in the Cote-des-Neiges, Cote-St-Luc and Snowdon areas creates the need to spend more money on their well-being.

Table 33: Jewish Elderly Population by District

District	65-74	75+	65+	Total Pop.	65+ %Tot
Chomedey	395	165	560	7460	7.4
Côte-des-Neiges	1745	1665	3420	9405	36.4
Côte-St-Luc	3540	1920	5455	20720	26.3
Hampstead	950	730	1690	7795	21.7
Mont-Royal	240	140	380	3125	12.2
NDG & Mtl West	920	595	1515	6530	23.2
Outremont	195	155	375	3035	12.4
Park/Centre Ville	625	350	955	4200	22.7
Ville St-Laurent	1005	310	1330	7890	16.9
Snowdon	980	1020	1995	4945	40.3
West Island	125	55	175	8800	2.0
Westmount	730	720	1455	7320	19.9
Rest of Mtl.	190	150	355	4995	7.1
Total Mtl CMA	11650	7995	19655	96235	20.4

C. Shahar

Unfortunately, one of the main problems of being over 65 is being or becoming poor. Many are below the poverty line, may just eke out a living, and are powerless to enjoy a full life in Montreal. The Jewish community is well-organized in helping the poor. Project Genesis, the food banks, the internal organizations (Jewish Family Services of Baron de Hirsch, Le Mercaz (food and clothing) and the Jewish Vocational Services) all try to help those in need.

"One out of five Jews in Montreal lived below the Statistics Canada poverty line or were marginal to it in the 1991 census".[2]

Table 34: Poor *Jewish Elderly (65+) by District—1986

District	Male Poor	Female Poor	Total Poor	Total 65+	% Total Poor
Chomedey	45	105	150	555	27.0
Cote-des-Neiges	400	785	1,185	3,420	34.6
Cote-st-Luc	285	710	995	5,455	18.2
Hampstead	115	195	310	1,690	18.3
Mont Royal	30	50	80	380	21.1
NDG & Mtl West	95	200	295	1,515	19.5
Outremont	45	60	105	375	28.0
Park/Center Ville	100	85	185	955	19.4
Ville St-Laurent	100	160	260	1,330	19.5
Snowdon	250	480	730	1,995	36.6
West Island	10	20	30	175	17.1
Westmount	15	95	110	1,455	7.6
Rest of Mtl.	15	95	135	355	38.0
Total Mtl	**1,585**	**3,010**	**4,595**	**19,650**	**23.4**

C. Shahar
*income of the household below $11,000 per year

The total population of Jews in Montreal has started to decline. The average age is increasing. What of the future? Looking at population projections for Canada, Canada's figures are startling for those over 65.

The estimates for Canada are
1996: 12.9%
2001: 13.8%
2011: 16.4%
2021: 21.7%.

While the aging Jewish community in Montreal is at 22.8% in 1991, the rest of Canada is at 10.9%.[3]

Will the people over 65 in the Jewish community reach 30-35%? How can the community not disintegrate and be unable to look after its own people? Can the Community have 25-30% over the poverty line, a declining population base, a declining economic base, and survive? Many epic decisions must be made by the Jewish community to face these problems, especially with regard to its older citizens who have given their community so much.

Notes

1. Layton, Irving. Direct Quote from "Irving Layton" by Daniel Goodwin *Gazette* March 5, 1995, PCI & C4.
2. Torczyner, J. "To be poor and Jewish in Canada" from *Can. Jewish Mosaic*, p. 20.
3. Perreault, J. & Decos M. *Population Projections 1989-2011*. Government of Canada, Ottawa Stats. 1990. Gov't Doc. CA1 ST 91-520. p.30&40.

References

Arnold, Janice. "FCJA Study Reports on Aging Population." *C N News*. Oct. 7, 1995, p. 5.

Bourbeau, Robert & Légaré, Jacques *Evolution de la Mortalité au Canada et au Québec 1831-1931*. Montreal, 1982. HB1360 Q4 B68.

Choinière, Robert & Robitaille, Norbert "The aging of ethnic groups in Québec" in *Ethnic Demography* S. Halli (ed.) Ottawa 1990. HB 3529 E84.

Cohen, S.M. (ed.) *Perspectives in Jewish Population Research*. Boulder, 1984. DS 143 P467.

Davids, Leo. "Canadian Jewry: Some Recent Census Findings." *AJYB* 85: 191-201. E184 J5 A6

Driedger, Leo & Chappell, Neena. *Aging & Ethnicity: Toward an Interface*. Toronto,1987. HQ1061 D779.

Kahan, Arcadius, *Essays in Jewish Social History* Chicago, 1986. DS 140.5 K33.

Kalbach, W.E., & McVery. *The Demographic Bases of Can. Soc*. Toronto, 1971. HB3529K3X, See chapter #7.

Layton, Irving. Direct Quote from "Irving Layton" by Daniel Goodwin *Gazette* March 5, 1995, PCI & C4.

McDaniel, Susan. *Canada's Aging Population* Toronto,1986. HQ 1064 C2M 134C.

Northcott, Herbert C. 'The aging of Canada's population: an up-date from the 1981 census." *Can. St. in Pop*. vol. 11 #1, 1984 29-45. HB848 C 36.

_____. *Changing Residence: Geographic Mobility of Elderly Canadians*. Scarborough, 1988, HB 1989 N67.

Overbeek, J. *Population & Canadian Society*. Toronto, 1980. HB 3529 O93

Polak, Monique. "A Friend in New Land." *Gazette*. Feb. 27, 1996, p. B4 (on Russian Jews).

Perreault, J. & Decos M. *Population Projections 1989-2011*. Government of Canada, Ottawa Stats. 1990. Gov't Doc. CA1 ST 91-520. p.30-43.

Richler, Mordecai. *Home Sweet Home*. Montreal, 1984, p.289 Quote from M. Himes.

Schmelz, V.O. et al. (ed.) *Studies in Jewish Demography: Survey from 1972-1980* N.Y. 1983. DS143 S77

Shahar, Charles. *Jewish community population statistics in Montreal*. FCJA, Montreal, 1989.

Spiegelman, M. "Longevity of Jews in Canada 1940-42" *Population Studies* 1948, 2: 292-304.

Torczyner, J. "To be poor and Jewish in Canada" from *Can. Jewish Mosaic*, p. 177-191.

Torczyner, J. "The Elderly" p. 204-207, "The Persistence of Invisible Poverty among Jews," p. 177-181, McGill Consortium.

Wilkins, Russell *L'espérance de vie par Quartier à Montréal 1976* Apr. 1979. Inst. for Research on Public Policy #3

The Economist. "The economics of Ageing" Jan. 27, 1996, Survey 16 pages.

Globe and Mail "Poverty rates high in Quebec, study says" June 26, 1996 p. B2. Showing Montreal figures at 22% in 1991 statistics.

CHAPTER 15

ASSOCIATIONS AND ORGANIZATIONS

Arriving in a city that had separate French and English community systems, the Jews set up their own similar structures and organizations based on their particular cultural needs.

It is hard to imagine the extensive network of the Jewish community and their long-time feeling for Kehillah—the self-help assembly that thrives when each community arrives in a new unfamiliar place. The Hebrew Philanthropic Society was the first official organization to aid Jews and was founded in 1848. Baron de Hirsch Institute, the Hebrew Free Loan Association, and Jewish Immigration Aid Services are other founding groups in their fields.

As the community grew, an umbrella association, now incorrectly called the Federation C.J.A. [Communities Jewish Agencies ?] (should be called Federation of Montreal's Jewish Agencies), became the main vehicle for community support. It looks over many aspects of community life, and presently has twenty-two main agencies. It also helps fund the Canadian Jewish Congress and sends a substantial proportion of its collections to Israel.

The community also helps to support seven health-related organizations and the YM-YWHA—each having its own budget. There are numerous smaller organizations and associations that receive monies from donations and grants.

The parochial school system has many centers in synagogues, while grade school and high school classes and specialized schools for higher learning in Judaism have their own buildings. The funding for this education comes from the community, with help from the Province of Quebec.

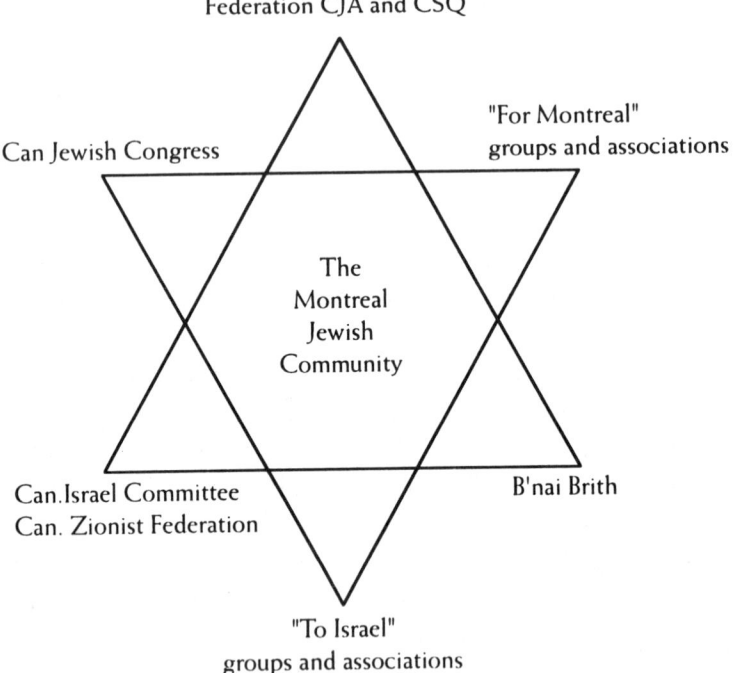

The Federation has an annual campaign and the CSQ's (Communauté Sépharade du Québec) campaign is integrated with it.

"To Montreal" groups associations. These bodies give directly to needy Montreal associations. A list is in the Appendix.

B'nai Brith—an international fraternal and service organization. Works to further Jewish life in Canada and Israel.

"To Israel" groups and Associations. These alliances give directly to schools, universities and other organizations in Israel without going through the Jewish Agency or the Fed. CJA. A list is in the Appendix.

Canada-Israel Committee. This group dominated by right-wing Zionists has looked after some contacts between

the two countries. Lately, they are trying to carve out a larger niche within the Community's other organizations.
Canadian Zionist Federation. This organization brings all segments of the Zionist movement together and promotes Israel.
Canadian Jewish Congress. It supports Jews in Canada and defends issues that are national in scope.

As each group is hoping to gain more adherents and monies and enlarge their platform there is a constant overlapping of responsibilities and energies.

Each group has a Board of Governors, Board of Directors, and Executive Committee. Occasionally, there is an election. In 1995, there was an open election for the C.J.C. presidency and the regional heads. The C.J.C. has been cross-Canada oriented. It almost changed its ways as the head of the Zionist C.I.C. fought and almost won the election through mischievous means. Ms. Goldie Hershorn won and is continuing the C.J.C. priorities, and the Canadian Jewish Congress was saved from being subordinated to the Zionist causes.[1]

Notes
1. Arnold, Janice "Hershorn wins CJC Presidency" *C.J. News* May 18, 1995, p. 3.

References
Arnold, Janice "Hershorn wins CJC Presidency" *C.J. News* May 18, 1995, p. 3.
Block, Irwin. "CJC President's 16 vote win fuels bitter feelings" *Gazette* May 16, 1995, p. A3.
Plaut, Gunther. "Goldie Hershorn's Task" *Canadian Jewish News* July 1, 1995, p. 10.
Sclick, Abel (editor). *History of B'nai Brith in Eastern Canada*. Toronto, 1964.
Canadian Jewish Congress "Fifty Years of service 1919-1969". *Canadian Jewish Congress* 1969
Appendix — Lists p,181-185.

CHAPTER 16

THE MONEY WEB

A group of YMHA runners, called the Wolfpack, run and enjoy the environment of the Mount Royal Mountain Park. Recently, they raised 7000 dollars and gave the money to the National Fund of Canada to plant trees in Israel.

In Judaism, there is an obligation to give. The credo of "helping someone to better himself/herself" is carried to great lengths and bestows great honour (Hebrew= Tzedakah)

The great Jewish philosopher, Maimonides described the different levels of giving or charity—

The lowest is he who gives unwillingly;

Then comes he who gives cheerfully, but not enough;

Then he who gives enough, but not until he is asked;

Then he who gives before being asked, but gives directly to the poor man;

The next classification: The poor man knows from whom he takes, but the giver does not know who is receiving;

Then the giver knows to whom he gives, but the receiver does not know the giver;

Then the giver does not know to whom he gives, nor does the poor man know from whom he receives; then comes

The highest form of charity is to strengthen the hand of the poor man by giving him a loan, joining him in partnership, or training him out of his poverty, to help him establish himself.[1]

As the Montreal Jewish community became stronger economically, this strength coincided with the growth of Israel. This simultaneous development and the strong Zionist presence in Montreal gave organizations in Montreal and Israel the chance to receive donations from Jewish Montrealers. The Money Web came into existence.

Anyone can give their own money to anyone. But on an individual and a more personal basis, a person born in a Montreal hospital, educated in a high school, a CEGEP (a Government-funded college), and then a Montreal university, having a successful career in Montreal, using Medicare, sending children through the same system, and wishing to donate—where does their philanthropy go? Maybe to Montreal, but quite often to Israel. Personal satisfaction, peer pressure, diasporic guilt, or dissatisfaction with Quebec's political and cultural climate? Each person has their own agenda.

There must be a way to redress this imbalance to give more to Montreal organizations and peoples as the infrastructure of our education, our health organizations, and our organizations for helping the needy must be funded. Concordia University, University of Montreal, and McGill University all need endowments for professorial chairs, new buildings and pure donations to erase their debt, such as the recent endowments of Harriet and Abe Gold and the Alexander/Goldfarb families who gave one million dollars each to McGill. The hospitals constantly need new labs and equipment; schools need new computers and books; and the immigrants need funding until they get above the poverty line.

Table 35: Fed. C.J.A. Collections 1987, 92-95. (in millions)

	1987	1992	1993	1994	1995
Total raised	30.0(?)	29.5	30.6	30.4	30.6
going to					
Local	10.9	11.6	12.4	12.5	12.7
C.J.C.	2.7	2.7	2.8	2.5	2.5
Israel	16.4	12.2	12.4	12.4	12.3
Expenses	?	3.0	3.0	3.0?	3.0?

Annual reports Fed CJA

Table 36: Revenue Stream of Fed. C.J.A.

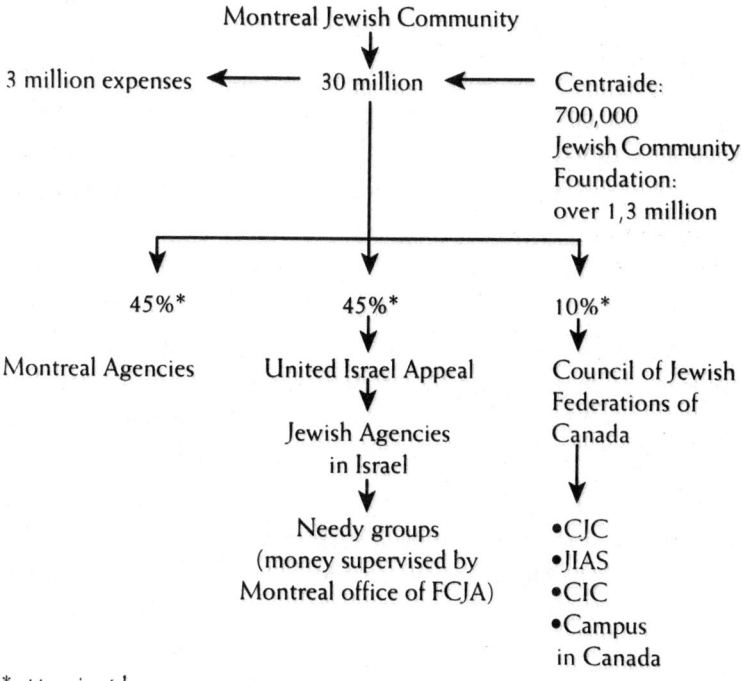

* approximately.

Locally, the Fed. C.J.A. money is tightly parcelled out to twenty-two agencies that cover some of the needs of the community—some say too thinly—in different groupings. For example, in 1994: Jewish Continuity, $3 million; Service for Seniors, $1.85 million; Family and Children's Services, $3.6 million; and Community Services, $3.4 million.[2]

The endowments and assets of the Fed. C.J.A. are not shown on their Annual Report.

Centraide, a United Appeal that is funded by all Montrealers, gives approximately $700,000 each year to the Fed. CJA with an agreement allowing Centraide to be the only agency to make employee deductions in companies. The Jewish Community Foundation gives at least $1.3 million directly to the Fed. CJA designated for Montreal causes. These two gifts allow the Federation to shift the corresponding amounts received from others to donations to Israel.

The money that goes to Israel from the FCJA constitutes the fifth largest amount from any Jewish community in the World. This gives the Montreal Federation clout in many Israel-connected agencies and decisions, and the Federation keeps close watch on these monies. This accounts for the main reason for the numerous dignitaries coming from Israel and in keeping a Consular office in Montreal. Most of the monies going to Israel go directly to Project Renewal in Beersheva, Jewish Montreal's twin town (Yeruham was the first), where Montrealers have control over the projects. Other monies go to the United Jewish Appeal which gives money to the Jewish Agency for Israel. They help immigration, absorption, rural settlement and education —and also youth aliyah here in Montreal where the Federation has no direct control. Some money goes to the Joint Distribution Committee that aids poor communities throughout the world.[3]

Joining the debate on Israeli aid is Matti Golan[4] (whose character Israel says to Judah)—"The main reason you send money, it seems to me, is that you still don't feel safe in the country you live in. No matter how much a part of American (Canadian) society you feel, you can't rule out the possibility of unexpected developments.... I'm (Israel) your insurance company and you make your payments to me just as you do as on your home and life insurance?"

Is the aid needed in Israel? This aid worldwide is now less than 1% of Israel's gross domestic product. The per capita income in Israel is now $16,600. While giving donations fosters solidarity with the Jewish State, a bond that should never be broken, it does not buy the right to interfere in the life and politics of those in Israel.[5]

Others say, "it is a fundamental right for Jews to contribute to Israel"[6] and "Raising funds for Israel is not charity but a means, for those who will not make aliyah to `contribute' to Israel and bear their share of the responsibility in areas of common concern".[7]

The number of private groups that back organizations in Israel is almost infinite. The list in the appendix, though incomplete, shows the diversity. For example, the Montreal Chapter of Canadian Friends of Tel Aviv University held their annual meeting on Oct. 17, 1994 to report that they had raised $2.3 million in 1994. This covered cancer research, architecture, biology. The group was unfortunately allied, though for a good cause, to the politically expedient Mulroney Institute of Canadian-Israeli Relationships. The Canadian Friends have a staffed office in Montreal and the executive goes to an annual Canadian meeting every year. Amazingly, in 1995, it was in Stowe, Vermont, U.S. of A!

Nationally, the Fed. C.J.A. funds go to the head office of the Canadian Jewish Congress which pools all monies and then parcels it out to their districts in need, the Jewish Immigration Aid Service, and Campus groups in universities and colleges in Canada.

The C.J.C.-Quebec in Montreal, for example, funds the Canadian Jewish Archives (once headed by D. Rome, now by Ms. J. Rosen) which is a trove of information for research. In 1993, the C.J.C.Q. held a plenary with subjects concerning Montreal's Jews—Unity vs. Separation of Canada, Media relations, Youth challenges in Quebec, Israel viewed from Diaspora, civilization and Human Rights, and Future of Quebec Education. The National Plenary Assembly was held on May 14-15, 1995, in Montreal. In 1995, Quebec region, newly headed by Jack Jedwab, had the above priorities and the task of combating the "Yes" vote in the '95 Quebec referendum, with C.J.C.'s pro-unity stand on federalism.

Another type of charity is the money coming from foundations. Much of this money is given to the Fed. C.J.A.(I was unable to find out if this money is designated or goes into the general appeal.) There are 71 active Montreal Jewish Foundations. The information of these foundations is dated due to slow data retrieval and publishing, but it gives one an idea of their scope.

Table 37: *Montreal Foundation Giving Stream*

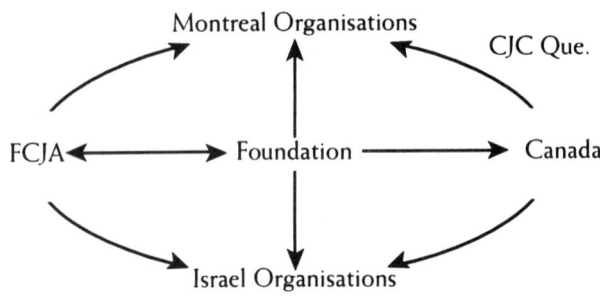

Table 38: Selected Foundations (over 1 million in Assets (1993)

	Assets (millions)	Grants (millions)
Bronfman Families	70.5	5.4
Cummings	7.8	0.9
Chastel (C. Bronfman)	133.6	13.6
Eldee	49.5	3.1
Ellen	1.7	0.2
Gelmont	10.0	0.4
Frankel	10.0	0.1
Jewish Community Foundation	26.0	1.9
Kaufmann	7.0	0.3
Kolber	5.0	0.4
Levitt	2.5	0.2
Ludmer	1.2	0.1
Pollack	3.2	0.2
Steinberg	7.7	1.5
Strauss	2.3	0.2
Victor	2.6	0.1

Canadian Center for Philanthropy 1995

There are family groups that do not enter into the Money Web. These donate in their way and without the resulting publicity living, as they do outside the whorl of the Web. This concept is accepted by the Community as these families are the ones who shoulder another wave of small donations, most of which are given without receiving tax receipts. Many 'poor' Jews from Israel and others from the New York / New Jersey area come to Montreal looking for small donations. An unknown amount is given in this way but it is substantial.

The following is an example of community giving: The Hebrew Free Loan Association, founded in 1911, has assets of 4 million dollars built up by donations and loan repayments over the years. Interest-free loans, secured by three guarantors in the Association, are given to Jews in the community to start or strengthen small businesses. The Association's quiet help gives the donors the highest form of charity.

I was unable to obtain statistics on the monies donated to synagogues and the cemeteries for their on-going needs.

The Money Web seems all encompassing. Golan put it well:

> "A driving force is this money machine—the urge to *schnor* which is an expectation of charity based on a pretension of merit—to the point where it becomes a way of life."[8]

Charitable giving of the Jewish Community in Montreal is staggering—$70 to $80 million a year. This shows in a very positive way that the Jewish Community donates to help Montrealers. Each geographic or ethnic community in Montreal should learn and act from this model.

Notes

1. Neusner, Jacob. *Tzedakah: Can Jewish philanthropy buy Jewish survival?* Atlanta 1990 BM523,5 C43N48. p.
2. Shahar, Charles. "A Survey of Jewish Life in Montreal", *Fed. J.C.S. of Montreal Dec.* 1996. p.16-17.
3. Shahar, Charles. "A Survey of Jewish Life in Montreal", *Fed. J.C.S. of Montreal Dec.* 1996. p.12-13.
4. Golan, Matti. *With friends like you: What Israelis really think about American Jews.* New York 1992 E184 J5 G594. p.52.
5. Beilin, Yossi. "Is Aid Needed in Israel?" *N.Y. Times.* Feb. 1, 1994, P.A.S. p.A3
6. Reiner, Michael. "Bringing Israel and Diaspora Together" C.J. News. Aug. 15 94, p. 7.
7. Leket, Yehiel. "Continue financial aid to Israel" *Canadian Jewish News* Apr. 21, 1994, p. 18.
8. Golan, Matti. *With friends like you: What Israelis really think about American Jews.* New York 1992 E184 J5 G594. p. 49.

References

Arenson, Karen "Donations to a Jewish Philanthropy Ebb" *N.Y. Times* Dec. 27, 1995, p. A10.

Arnold, Janice "Hershorn wins CJC Presidency" *C.J. News* May 18, 1995, p. 3.

Beilin, Yossi. "Is Aid Needed in Israel?" *N.Y. Times*. Feb. 1, 1994, P.A.S.

Beilin, Yossi. "New Diaspora—Israel relationships suggested" *CJN News*. Dec 1, 1994, p. 1.

Block, Irwin. "CJC President's 16 vote win fuels bitter feelings" *Gazette* May 16, 1995, p. A3.

Canadian Center for Philanthropy *Canadian Directing of Foundations*. Toronto 1994. LB 2339C3H6 1994

Carlson, Martin. *Why People Give*. New York, 1968. BJ1533G4C37

Cohen, Elaine. "Charles Bronfman interviews—Investment in Israel doubly rewarding", *C.J.N.* Feb. 15, 1995. p.27.

Golan, Matti. *With friends like you: What Israelis really think about American Jews*. New York 1992 E184 J5 G594

Jaffe, Eliezer, "Whose Jewish Agency is it?" *Jerusalem Post*. Apr. 8, 1995, p. 7.

Leket, Yehiel. "Continue financial aid to Israel" *Canadian Jewish News* Apr. 21, 1994, p. 18.

Neusner, Jacob. *Tzedakah: Can Jewish philanthropy buy Jewish survival?* Atlanta 1990 BM523,5 C43N48.

Plaut, Gunther. "Goldie Hershern's Task" *Canadian Jewish News* July 1, 1995, p. 10.

Reiner, Michael. "Bringing Israel and Diaspora Together" C.J. News. Aug. 15 94.

Shahar, Charles. "A Survey of Jewish Life in Montreal", *Fed. JC.S. of Montreal* Dec. 1996

Weiss, David. "The Jewish social services in Quebec—A Historical Survey, 1863-1984" *Intervention* 69 (1984): 11-16.

PART IV

BIASES

CHAPTER 17

ANTI-SEMITISM

Jews have suffered for centuries under Islam and Christianity. With the gradual separation of state from institutional religion, this religious anti-Judaism has developed into racial anti-Semitism. Few goyim understand Judaism, and those who are anti-Semitics prey on this mystery. "Suspicion which can shade off into hostility".[1] Stories about plots to overthrow the Christian civilization, rumours of the Jews acting out blood libel, continued teachings that Jews killed Jesus Christ, cartoons of the devil and a wicked Jew, and the mere fact that the Jews are seen as different perpetuate prejudice and hate mongering. As history teaches, it is easy to blame someone 'foreign' for one's own failings.

Every country has victimized the Jews. Even after World War II and the Holocaust, there have been attacks. For example, 210,000 Polish refugees from Russia went back to Poland to live. In Kielce in July 1946, a pogrom and killings occured resulting in a panicked massive migration, 100,000 to Palestine in '46-'47 and 110,000 to the West. In 1996, there are only 5000 Jews in Poland and there is heightened anti-Semitism there even with Polish democracy and freedom of the press.

The reaction by any Jewish community to attacks is to put up the barricades or face the perpetrator head-on. Most societies in these situations just compromise against any slight.

Dershowitz describes his "constant state of preparedness for potential persecutors: (I call it my) Holocaust Mentality".[2]

In Quebec, rampant anti-Semitism was the norm in both the French and English societies. In the 1940's, I remember on a visit near Ste-Agathe a sign saying: "No dogs, No Jews." A hand bill from the mid-30's found in Ste-Agathe:

NOTICE
Jews are not wanted
Here in Ste-Agathe
Scram while the going is good
AVIS
Les juifs ne sont pas désirés ici
Ste-Agathe est un village canadien français
et nous le garderons ainsi.

Public Archives of Canada #PA107943

Often you can equate Nazism and extreme nationalism with Anti-Semitism there are interesting books on the subject documenting their fanatics such as the Adrien Arcand (National Social Christian Party), Joseph Ménard (owner of "Le Patriote"), and Salluste Lavery, K.C. (Member of the Native Sons of Canada).

Then there are the stories of Jews being denied admission to universities, private clubs, and business firms.

In 1991, I conducted a survey of 35 working French Canadians who lived in Lachine, Lasalle, Cote-St-Paul and Verdun:

Questions: Were you taught	Yes	No	Do Not Remember
1. "That Jesus Christ was killed by Jews"	19	13	3
2. "Jews were killed in the past for Blood Libel"	6	20	9
3. "Were you taught by priests or nuns?"	30	5	0

All those answering yes in #1 and #2 were taught by priests. This is another indication of the religious intolerance and its attacks on Judaism that is embedded in many parts of Quebec's society —another example of self-perpetuating tribalism.

The Canadian Jewish Congress and the B'nai Brith continually express their stand on anti-semitism at any time when there is hint of the problem. Mr. J. Parizeau's comment after losing the '95 Referendum, (he blamed the "money and ethnic vote"), wasn't just a hint of anti-semitism; it was a racist attack by the Premier of Quebec. Anti-Semitism is still rampant in Montreal, but people now hide it better until stress brings it out.

I am reminded of a witticism—

> A skinhead is swaggering down the sidewalk while in the opposite direction walks a quiet, elegantly dressed Jew.
> They bump into each other accidentally.
> "Swine!" exclaims the skinhead.
> The Jew bows slightly and replies "Horowitz".[3]

A search for a new mental approach for all Jews is contemplated by Dershowitz: "a demand for a new Jewish state of mind capable of challenging the conventional wisdom that Judaism is more adaptive to persecution and discrimination than it is to an open, free and welcoming society — that Jews paradoxically need enemies in order to survive, that anti-Semitism is what has kept Judaism alive."

Notes

1. Naipaul, Shiva. *An Unfinished Journey*. London, 1986. PR 9272.9 N3 U5. "... Suspicion which can shade off into hostility." p. 1.
2. Dershowitz, Alan M. *Chutpah*, Toronto, 1991. p. 136.
3. Naiman, Arthur. *Every Goy's Guide to Common Jewish Expressions*. N.Y. 1992. p. 42
4. Dershowitz, Alan M. *The Vanishing American Jews: in Search of Jewish Identity for the Next Century*. Boston 1997. Especially Chapter #3 — "Anti-Semitism in the Twenty-First Century".

References

Arnold, Janice. "Anti semitic Acts Worry Quebec Jews:B.B. Audit". *C.J.N.* March 20, 1997.

Betcherman, Lita-Rose. *The Swastika and the Maple Leaf*. Toronto 1975 FC548F3B47

Brym, Robert J. "The Distribution of Anti-Semitism in Canada in 1984" *Viewpoints* XIV #6 1991: 1-2 Dec. 6, 91.

Cohn, Norman, R.C. *Warrant for Genocide: The Myth of the Jewish world - conspiracy and the Protocols of the Elders of Zion*. New York,1967. DS 145 P7 C6

Davies, Alan T. (ed.) *Anti-Semitism in Canada*. Waterloo, 1992. DS 146 C7 A78 1992.

Delisle, Esther. *The Traitor and the Jews: Anti-Semitism and Extreme Right-wing Nationalism in Quebec 1929-1939*. Montreal, 1993. FC 2924.9 N3 D 4413. Also see CJN Apr. 1, 93, p. 6 = Interview.

Dershowitz, Alan M. *Chutzpah*, Toronto, 1991.

_____. *The Vanishing American Jews: in Search of Jewish Identity for the Next Century*, Boston, 1997.

Dobkowski, David. *The Tarnished Dream - The Basis of American Anti-Semitism*. Westport, Conn., 1979. DS 146 U6 D6.

Langlois, Andre. "... Segregation residentielle à Montréal" *Canadian Geog.* 29: 197-206, 1985.

Libman, Robert & Scheinberg, Stephen. " A Worried Minority ". *Montreal Gazette*, March1, 1997, p.B5.

Littman, S. *Quebec's Jews: vital citizens or eternal strangers*. 35 pages. Toronto, 1991. [Simon Wiesenthal Center Report].

Naiman, Arthur. *Every Goy's Guide to Common Jewish Expressions*. N.Y. 1992.

Naipaul, Shiva. *An Unfinished Journey*. London, 1986. PR 9272.9 N3 U5. "... Suspicion which can shade off into hostility." (p. 1).

Robin, Martin. *Shades of Right: Nativist and Fascist Politics in Canada 1920-40* Toronto 1992 FC549R6

Rome, David. *The Plamondon Case and S.W. Jacobs*. Montreal, 1982. DS146Q4R6 (Part I and Part II).

Roy, Raoul. *Lettres aux juifs de Montréal: le secret des juifs*. Montreal, 1979. FC 2950 J5 R6.

Seidel Judith. *The Development and Social Adjustment of the Jewish Community in Montreal*. Mathesis, 1939. AS 42 M3 1939 S45.

Shahar, Charles " A Survey of Jewish Life in Montreal". *Fed. JCS of Montreal*. Dec. 1996. In Shahar's 1996 survey only 15% felt that there is a 'great deal' of anti-semitism while 62% of the survey stated that there is 'some' semitism. A problem in the survey was the 20% that didn't know or did not respond.

Silcox, C.E. *Catholics Jews and Protestants—A Study of Relationships in the U.S. and Canada*. 1934. BL 2520 S54.

Taguieff, Pierre André (editor) *Protocoles des sages de Sion*. Berg. Int.—Paris 1992.

Trachtenberg, Joshua. *The Devil and the Jews: The Medieval Conception of the Jews and its Relation to Modern Anti-Semitism*. New Haven, 1943. DS 145 T7 1966.

Weinfeld, Morton. "The Jews of Quebec: Perceived Anti-Semitism, Segregation and Emigration". *Jew J. of Soci*. vol. 22, #1 Jan. '80: p. 5-20.

Zand, Nicole. "Another twist in the great Jewish plot that never was". *Manchester Guardian Weekly*. May 10, 1992, p. 15.

Anti-Semitism in Canada. DS 146 C2—all publications on this call number.

CHAPTER 18

THE HOLOCAUST

After many years of study in political science, profuse numbers of articles read, and innumerable serious conversations, I really have only a veneer of knowledge about the Holocaust. But in writing this book, I had to come to grips with the horror, so I read some first hand accounts. I tried to implant myself into the Jewish milieu. I really haven't succeeded. All I can say is that tears of grief are in my eyes.
I read articles (e.g. Brenner, Margalit, Hertzberg) and books (Zuckerman, Borowski, Appelfeld) in order to work towards an understanding. Then, at 9:27 p.m. Oct. 30, 1993 in a quiet corner of the McLennan Library, as I was looking up population trends, I opened up Volume 13 of David Rome's 'Clouds in the Thirties' not really knowing what it was about. As I turned the pages I was shocked—I got a cold feeling of numbness. I broke into a sweat as I read this first chapter written by Oskar Strawczynski.
Mr. Leo Strawczynski, his son, has kindly given me permission to print this chilling account from *Ten Months in Treblinka*.

Ten Months in Treblinka ©
Chapter 1
It was the day after Succoth, October 5, 1942. The morning was bright and sunny. Although utterly exhausted after twenty-four hours in the tightly packed cattle cars, we shivered with terror when the train stopped

and we heard frightful shouts: "Out, Out..." Whips fly over our heads... In the eyes of my wife I recognize that finally even she has begun to believe the horrible rumours about the gas factory beyond Malkinia. I can see that now she regrets not having agreed to my plan to hide with the children in our neighbour's hideout. She could not bring herself to believe all the malicious talk. She had wanted to believe that as long as we were together, no evil could reach her or our dear children.

We run out as fast as we can to avoid the whips lashing overhead, and find ourselves on a long, narrow platform, crowded to capacity. All familiar faces—neighbours and acquaintances. The dust so tremendous, it obscures the sunlight. A smell of charred flesh stifles the breath. Unwittingly, I catch a glimpse of the mountains of clothing, shoes, bedding and all kinds of wares that can be seen over the fence. But there is no time to think.... The dense mass of people is pushed toward and jammed through a gate.

At this moment I just have one thought—not to lose my dearest ones in all this chaos. I succeed in keeping together my wife, two beautiful children, mother and father. Little do I know that these are our last moments together, that behind that gate we would be torn apart and we would never see each other again...

In that great tumult I do not notice that the work on the platform, such as clearing the people and leftover luggage from the trains, and herding and pushing the crowd toward the gate, is performed by a detachment of around thirty Jewish men wearing blue armbands. This is the detachment of "Blues" commanded by Kapo Mayer. On the platform there are also S.S. men, the Ukrainian "Wachmener" (Watchmen) of Treblinka and also the policemen and guard escorting the train. When the last of the transport passes through the gate, and the wagons are cleared, the escort returns to their wagon and the train leaves the camp. All this happens very quickly, and I noticed the details only later, while working in Treblinka.

Behind the gate we find ourselves in quite a large square with barracks on two sides. Opposite the fence and the gateway through which we had passed is a fence with a small entrance in the corner. This is the gate to the "Alley of Death" which leads to the "baths" in Camp 2. Down this Alley, completely naked, they took their last walk—my dear wife and children, father, mother, brothers and sisters, together with millions of Jewish men and women.... They never came out of the "bath". Their sacred bodies were heaped on stretchers and thrown into the infernal fires.

Later, when I was working on the rooftops of Treblinka, I had many opportunities to watch that last walk of our naked, unfortunate people: Mothers holding their little ones in their arms, older children at their sides, young girls with their hair already shorn, covering their breasts with their hands, or several together, arms linked— all running as quickly as possible through the aisle of Germans and Ukrainians who laugh, and mock them. Quite often, one or another of the victims was struck on the head with a whip or rifle butt and collapsed in a stream of blood. Those were horrible scenes from hell.

I return to the moment when we entered the so-called Transport Square. As we take our first steps we hear shouts that freeze our blood. I stop thinking or feeling. We know only one thing: these are our last moments together. The shouts become louder and more penetrating: "Men to one side, women to the other."

We are completely confused by the lightning speed and terrible noise. I do not, I cannot, say a single word, not even a final farewell to my loved ones. I just hear the sigh of my beloved wife and her last words: "That's it." No one can know how much despair and anguish those words contained. To me they are an abyss of sorrow. I still hear those words ringing in my ears and I will surely not forget them to the last moments of my life.

Writing these words I once again relive the sorrow of our parting. I cannot express the feelings raging within me. Fresh tears well up and the warm forest ground soaks up the hot stream from my eyes.

But there, on that sorrowful Transport Square, there is no time for tears or feelings. I scarcely have time to hand my wife the carefully hidden blanket for the children. A brutal hand grasps my shoulder and I am hurled to the other side of the Square. I manage to stay with my gentle father. The place is packed with people. On one side are women with small children, on the opposite side, men, forced to kneel. In the middle there are S.S. men, Ukrainians with weapons in their hands as well as a group of about forty men with red armbands. These are Jews—the detachment of "Reds". In Treblinka slang they are called "Chevra Kedisha" (Society for Last Rites).

Kapo Yurek was their leader, a Warsaw rickshaw driver, so corrupt and debauched, no deed was too foul for him. This brute would not hesitate to take aside a girl, already naked, on her march to the "bath". Promising to save her, he would do the worst, then push her back into the line. He is dressed elegantly, as that type of person could easily afford to be in Treblinka. He works his whip frequently and with gusto on Jewish heads. As foul and corrupt as he was, his language was even worse. The vernacular of the Warsaw underworld was nothing new in Treblinka. There were great artists in that field, but no one could surpass Yurek. In short, he was quite a notable member of Treblinka's aristocracy. Most of the "Reds" were recruited from the Warsaw underworld, and did not fall far short of their Kapo.

Most prominent among all in the Square is a German officer, a stout man with a short beard, mounted on a beautiful brown horse. He moves haughtily on his horse, in the middle of the Square. At a certain point he turns toward the kneeling men and shouts: "Craftsmen out!" A number of men step out. Most of them, however, are sent back. Only a few are stood aside, where an S.S. man makes a further selection, and groups the remaining men in threes. I am kneeling beside my father. I do not even say a single word to my father.

Among the men with the red armbands, I notice a familiar face. At first, I cannot recall who he is, but then I recognize him. He is Aaron Berliner, a worker from the Czestochowa Jewish Community. He too has noticed me. He motions me to come over to him. I stand up, take my father's hand and try to take my bundle also. He orders me to leave my bundle, and orders my father to kneel as before. Aaron leads me to the mounted German. The German looks me over and asks: "What's your trade?" "Tinsmith" I say. He motions me toward the selected group, where Aaron leads me. Now I am completely alone, also parted from my father, without a kiss, without a single farewell...

The group grows to about sixty men—no women. A man of about thirty approaches us. He is tall and broad with strong muscular legs and black hair—a young giant. This is Kapo Rakowski. He shouts a command and leads us away in military formation. Marching through the remaining mass of people I scan the women's side. Perhaps I can catch a last glimpse of my loved ones, perhaps I will again see my two little angels. I do not find them—probably, they are in the barracks.

We are led to an enormous square, piled with mountains of bundles. In the distance is a tall embankment on which a watchman saunters back and forth, his rifle on his arm. From behind the embankment thick smoke bursts as from a volcano.

My brain is still foggy. I see and hear as in a dream. There are no people on the square. Kapo Rakowski leads us towards a mountain of clothing. We collapse against the mountain, exhausted and beaten down. The Kapo delivers a lecture. The words bounce off my ears. He talks about money: "We should give it away. Here you do not need money. You cannot buy a thing with it, anyway." I see people taking their money out and throwing it into valises. My thoughts are still hazy, they wander back to the ones left at the Transport Square. Suddenly, I break into hysterical tears. I bury my head in the mountain of clothing and remain there, sobbing, for a long time.

The square, quiet until now, suddenly becomes very noisy. I lift my head, look around, and see a most bizarre sight: Naked men with bundles pressed to their bodies are running through an aisle of guards, who whip them on to a horse's gallop. The victims jump up comically when their way is barred by a stick, or when they are whipped on their behinds. The route leads from the Transport Square to the large sorting square. The victims run around one of the mountains of clothing, throw their bundles onto it and, without stopping, run back to the Transport Square. This "dance macabre" has been going on now for over fifteen minutes. From the distance I recognize my neighbours. I see my neighbour Palacz being led to the Lazaret (field hospital), from where shortly afterwards, a shot is heard. Palacz, a rather weak, delicate young man, evidently could not pass the "training". I did not see my father, or any other men his age, among those running.

After depositing their bundles the breathless men are led through the small gate into the "Alley of Death", with their hands raised over their heads. At the gateway is a little hut. There the "Gold Jews" take the victims' valuables, money, and documents, "for deposit only"—until they return from the "bath". A special sign announces that there are no limitations on foreign exchange.

The crowd has passed through and there is silence for a few minutes.

Suddenly a smothered mass scream is heard from the distance—a-a-a... The scream does not last long, it becomes weaker and weaker until it dies away.... I know instinctively that this is the last cry of the unfortunate, condemned victims—among them my own, my loved ones—Again, I break into hysterical tears.

After every transport I heard this same last cry, making my blood run cold.

Even today, as I reread this chapter after having finished off the rest of this book, I am struck with a deep horror that I've never felt before—not at my own father's death, those two motorcyclists twitching after been hit by a car and helping and not being able to help them live, their blood all over me, or after seeing, close by, a suicide off Jacques Cartier Bridge—but this is worse by a degree I cannot express—a wanton act so much against what I feel life is. "Where was God?", you might ask.

References

Abley, M.."Our Souls are Tattooed". *Gazette.* Dec. 11, 1994, p. A1.
Allen, Woody. "Random Reflections of a Second-Rate Mind" *Tikkun* #5 #1 Jan./Feb. 1990 p. 13-15, p. 71.
Appelfeld, Aharon. *Badenheim 1939.* Boston, 1980.
Brenner, Rachel F. "A.M. Klein and Mordecai Richler: Canadian Responses to the Holocaust" *Journal of Can. Studies* vol. #24, #2 1989: 65-77.
Borowski, Tadeusz. *This way for the gas, Ladies.* Warsaw, 1959.
Elon, Amos. "The Politics of Memory." *N.Y. Review of Books.* Oct. 7, 1993, p. 3-5.
Gilbert, Martin. "Gold road to the gas chamber" in *Manchester Guardian Weekly* May 31, 92, p. 26.
Hertzberg, Arthur. "A life-long quarrel with God" *N.Y. Times Book Review.* p. 1 and 39-41.
Langer, L.L. *Admitting the Holocaust.* N.Y. 1995. D 804.3L358.
Margalit, Avishai "The uses of the Holocaust" *N.Y. Review of Books.* Feb. 17, '94: 7-10.
Segev, Tom. *The Seventh Million: The Israel and the Holocaust.* London, 1993.

Strawczynski, Oskar. "Ten months in Treblinka: memoirs of Oskar Strawczynski" vol. 13. *From Clouds in the Thirties*. Vol. 13, ed. David Rome. C.J. Congress, Montreal, 1981. P.I.-LXI. DS146C2 R65
Torczyner, J. "Holocaust Survivors" p. 55-57 from McGill Consortium (et al.)
Weinraub, B. *N.Y. Times* Nov. 10, 1994 p. C22 "Spielberg Recording Survivors' Stories".
Zuckerman, Yitzhak. *A Surplus of Memory: Chronicle of the Warsaw Ghetto Uprising*. Berkley,1993, D804.3 Z 7613.
"Explaining the Unthinkable" in *Economist*, Feb. 1, 92, p.103-4.
Montreal Institute for Genocide Studies. Concordia U.
Montreal Holocaust Centre, 5151 Cote-Ste-Catherine Rd., 345-2605
    Gazette Sept. 17, 94 P.I.1.
    CJN, Oct. 28, 93, p. 23.
    Gazette, Dec. 8,91, p. H4.
CJN Apr. 16, 92, p. 19—gives list of all the Holocaust survivor committees in Montreal.

CHAPTER 19

DUALISM

The Concept of Dualism

A person living in one country, having lived there for a length of time, having a home and being a citizen of that country, and wishing for the well-being of its citizens, establishs a relationship with the people of another country — investing time and money to help there. Furthermore, this person does this over and above what would be classified as a normal business or personal commitment. This person most probably has a feeling of split loyalties—a sort of dualism.

My paternal family arrived here four generations ago from Scotland and were originally from the Highlands near John O'Groats. On the maternal side and my paternal grandmother's side I'm descended from United Empire Loyalists from St. John and Kingston. I have neutral feelings for Scotland, Maine and Delaware after visiting them. I have no dualism—except with respect to Canada and Montreal.

First generations and second generations normally have a bond with their "home" country—for example, many of the Italians, Greeks and Portuguese whom I have known feel such a bond. As they become Canadianized, their roots gradually fade away, resulting in a diminishing sense of dualism.

The extremist Orthodox, both Ashkenazi and Sephardim, declare that the Land of Israel is the Holy Land. To them it must be populated and run under the Laws of Judaism, and one must, if able, make his/her Aliyah. They are only against the *State* of Israel because it has been run by the "atheist" Zionists, and they want to change this type of government to strengthen the religious participation in it.

The Zionists insist that every Jew is automatically a citizen of Israel and owes his first loyalty to Israel and not to the country of her/his residence. They are modernists who know that their dream will not be realized if the Orthodox control the government of Israel.

The non-Orthodox in the mainstream of each community are also in fear of assimilation; they want to support this motherland, but want to get on with their lives.

To sustain, to endure—the struggle to survive as a people (as a religion and a culture)—is present in the mind of every Jew. The importance of Israel cannot be overemphasized, even for those who want to remain in Diaspora. In 1908, Dubnow believed that in the past, the core of the Jewish survival was "the communal autonomy which enables the Jewish people [in different countries] to determine the course of its evolution under different circumstances and varying social and ethnic pressures" — even if it meant living in ghettos.

The Jewish Community in Montreal is affected by Dualism. It's like having two mothers and it is hard to serve these two mentors.

Even worse is the difficulty for non-Jews to determine if Jews have the ability to be loyal to their country while at the same time assisting and encouraging Israel with time, money and heart.

Dualism brings about questions from both sides—the Canadians suggesting that Jews do more for the people of Canada; the Israelis saying do more for your own people.[1] Does the Jew feel he is a guest in Canada? I think not, but it might cross his mind in Quebec. Dershowitz puts it bluntly—accusing North American Jews of being a Doppess[2]—one who watches, regrets what is happening but doesn't do anything but give money to suppress and cover the guilt of his dualism.

Outside Judaism, Jewish dualism is one of the causes of anti-semitism.

For dualism to be accepted in Montreal, the Jewish organizations within and without the Fed. CJA must educate the other ethnic groups (including the French) to realize that the Jews in Montreal are Montrealers first.

In a contest to explain "what Israel means to me" Josh Lambert, a student in Toronto wrote, "[Israel] creates a link among Jews worldwide, the political state of Israel gives Jews a means through which they can express their brotherhood." He adds: "Israel not only represents the ideals of Judaism; it also protects and serves Jewish religion and culture everywhere."[3]

The Jews in Montreal most certainly have this dualistic feeling for Israel. In 1997 one might ask about the anglophones of Quebec who feel a dual loyalty to Quebec and Canada and see Canada as their insurance policy against the radical nationalism (a stylized ethnic cleansing) in Quebec?

This dualism is different from, for instance, the Greeks who had a land and emigrated from it. They look back to their ancestors and relatives still living there and can go back to their homeland. Until 1948, Jews had no homeland. Their attachment to a homeland is completely different. They finally have one—they can finally smell the soil.

Dualism need not be a negative circumstance but must be explained better and more often to the public at large.

Notes

1. Dershowitz, Alan M. *Chutzpah* 1st Ed. Boston, 1991. p.244.
2. Dershowitz, Alan M. *Chutzpah* 1st Ed. Boston, 1991. p.16.
3. Lambert, Josh. "More than a Symbol of Jewish Faith." C.J.N. May 4, 1995, p. 12.

References

Bauer, Julien. "Diaspora and Israeli Jews: One People or Two?" 1994 *Viewpoints* 22; 2: p. 7-8.

Dershowitz, Alan M. *Chutzpah* 1st Ed. Boston, 1991.

Lambert, Josh. "More than a Symbol of Jewish Faith." *C.J.N.* May 4, 1995, p. 12.

Lipset, Seymour M. *American Pluralism and the Jewish Community.* New Brunswick, N.J. 1990.

Renbaum, Dafna. "Diminishing Returns." *Kol Emunah.* Summer 1992, p. 36-7.

Roth, Philip. *Operation Shylock.* N.Y. 1993.

Waxman, Chaim. "All in the Family: American Jewish Attachment to Israel." *Studies in Contemporary Jewry* 9, 1992, p. 134-149. (*especially paragraph on p. 145.)

Canadian Jewish News "Community Leaders urged to set new agenda with Israel" Sept. 1, 1994, p.30.

CHAPTER 20

NATIONALISM

All individuals carry within themselves frustrations, tensions, uncertainties, guilt feelings and a sense of deprivation [and alienation]. Nationalism is one way for them to overcome these stresses, purging themselves of guilt, to become fulfilled.[1]

Nationalism can be defined as a position held by an ethnic group with one language and a common past. This group is the dominant force in an area and feels it is the rightful guardian of its people. Other groups are tolerated with the hope that in time they will learn the language and customs and thereby become part of the system.

Feelings of Nationalism run deep.

Examples in times past: In Deuteronomy (7:6) Moses told the Jews they were "holy people" chosen by God to be a "special people above all people"; in On Duty (1, xvii, 57) Cicero to a meeting of the Senate. "Parents are dear, children are dear, as are our relatives and friends: but our fatherland embraces in itself all our love for everyone."

Quebec nationalism, different from the Roman Catholic ultramontaine domination of the French Canadian countryside, has been on the rise since the Quiet Revolution of the 1960s. This nationalism was transferred from a religious milieu to a political one, culminating in a victory of one nationalistic party, the Parti Québécois, in 1976. To counter the threat of separation, the provincial Liberal Party has become nationalistic too, though not as strident as the P.Q. Finally, with the election of the federal Bloc Québécois as the Official Opposition in Ottawa, all minorities in Quebec are questioning the policies of their French Canadian neighbours. Montreal, the only haven for the Jews of Quebec, is now stagnating, awaiting the effects of the 1995 Referendum, and the federal election of May 1997.

Quebec's nationalists are committed to investing the French Canadian majority in the province with absolute power over the province's politics, economy, and education. To gain this power, the movement sanctioned the anglophobia that has now grown to outrageous extremes in the separatist movement within Quebec nationalism and the federal Québec Bloc. "Separatist sentiment feeds on legitimate complaints about past injustices".[2]

Blinded to the eventual impact of separation on the Quebec society by visions of self-determination these stubborn advocates cover all major problems with nationalistic mists. The leaders have inculcated this mist into the separatist mind to a level that they are ready to believe their leader to endure the consequences no matter what the consequences are.

Linguistic paranoia was and is centered on the possible loss of the wide-spread usage that French now has in the province. Inculcated in the minds of the politicians is the concept that it is necessary to continue to have 80% of the population be francophone. In the 1950's and 1960's, Joy and after him Henripin, showed that with the loss of fertility, the continued immigration of anglophones, and the higher participation of the ethnic minorities in the election process, the francophones would find themselves, in the near future, in a position where the anglophones would attain absolute political power even with less than 50% of the population due to higher voting participation.[3]

The addition of the Moroccan French speaking Jews was welcomed by the nationalists—but not by the separatists, who felt that this minority within the Jewish minority would side with the Jewish community and vote against separatism. The upgraded immigration policies to keep the 80% level and gain voters resulted in the immigration by the Haitian, Vietnamese, and other French minorities. Many saw Canada as a stable place to live, and all look at the U.S. of A as still having "streets paved with gold".

The subject of Jewish dualism to the nationalist, let alone the separatist, has become an anathma because they just don't know how to regard the concept. This adds to their confusion about where to place their trust regarding the Jewish minority.

But the nationalist (read sovereignist) in Quebec espouses dualism also. They have ties to Canada. Unfortunately for Quebec and its populations, the separatists haven't realized that the rest of Canada will fervently reject any overtures of a separatist or sovereignist Quebec, for example the recent surge of the western Reform Party, and an economic and social crisis will result.[4] In early 1996, the possibilities of partition within Quebec have been raised to further complicate the issue. Steven Cummings opposed the move to make Quebec independent because "independence and the continued delegitimatization of the English language will slowly erode the vitality of the Jewish Community in Montreal".[5] If there is separation, and no further partition, the Jewish Community will disband in Montreal and move to Canada.

Notes
1. Shafer, Boyd. *Faces of Nationalism*. N.Y. 1972, p. 228.
2. Richler, Mordecai. "Tired of Separatism" *N.Y. Times* Oct. 31, 94: A-19.
 _____ "O Canada, O Quebec" *New Yorker*, May 30, 1994, p. 50.
3. Joy, Richard. *Languages in Conflict*. Montreal 1967. JL 25 J6.

4. Bryan, Jay. "Why is this economist worried?" *Gazette* May 13, 91: 10-11. p.11.

5. AJYB '95. p.221.

References

Bothwell, Robert. *Canada and Quebec: One Country Two Histories.* Vancouver, 1995. FC 2911 B67

Bryan, Jay. "Why is this economist is worried?" *Gazette* May 13, 91: 10-11.

Carens, J.H. (Ed.) *Is Quebec Nationalism Just?* Montreal, 1995. FC 2926.9 N3 187.

Cook, Ramsay. *Canada, Quebec and the Uses of Nationalism.* Toronto, 1995. FC97C66

Derriennic, J.P. *Nationalisme et democratie.* Montreal, 1995. FC2920N4D47

Duznow, Simon (1860-1941) *Nationalism and History.* ed. K. Spinson, Phila. 1961. DS 141.D76.

Handler, R. *Nationalism in the Politics of Culture in Quebec.* Madison, 1988. FC 2925.9N 3H29.

Henripin, Jacques. *La fin de la revanche des berceaux: qu'en pensent les Québécois?* Montreal 1974. HQ 766.5 C2 H45x

Henripin, Jacques. *Evolution demographie du Québec et ses regions 1966-1968.* Quebec 1969. Law HB 3530 Q4 H38.

Henripin, Jacques. "Majority at Risk." *Gazette* Feb. 21, 1995, A4.

Joy, Richard. *Languages in Conflict.* Montreal 1967. JL 25 J6.

Laforest, Guy. *Trudeau and the God of a Canadian Dream.* Montreal, 1995. JL 65 1992 C 3313

LaFrance, Louis. "Le demographie moraliste" *Le Devoir* Feb. 20, 1995, p. B1.

McRoberts, Kenneth. *Quebec: Social Change & Political Crisis (3rd Ed.)* Toronto, 1989. JL 242 M25X

Monahan, Patrick. *Cool Heads will Prevail: Assessing the Costs and Consequences of Quebec Separation.* Toronto, 1995. FC 2995.9 S4 M73.

_____. *If You Love This Country.* Notis BDC 3007.

Richler, Mordecai. "Tired of Separatism" *N.Y. Times* Oct. 31, 94: A-19.

_____ "O Canada, O Quebec" *New Yorker*, May 30, 1994, p. 50.

Romalis, Coleman. *Attitudes of Montreal Jews toward French Canadian Nationalism.* McGill, MA 1967. Folio 5029 3R65.

Shafer, Boyd. *Faces of Nationalism.* N.Y. 1972, p. 228.

Sheridan, Cris. "Two Solitudes: is it fear, loathing or misunderstanding that pits sovereignists against Jews?" *Mirror* oct. 14. 1996 p.8

Wills, Terrance. "Bloc Feud begins to build" *Gazette* Feb. 4, 94: B1.

Canadian Jewish News "Quebec not a threat to Jews" June 11, 92 p. 3.

PART V

WHAT IS TO BE DONE?

CHAPTER 21

EXTERNAL RAPPROCHEMENT

There should be no rights without obligations.

In Canada, minority groups arrived to find two separate antagonists already divided by race, religion and language so the minorities kept to themselves. The situation was one of ethnic pluralism—whereby each group has its own hierarchy, associations and religious affiliation, creating cultural enclaves. Later, the ethnic groups became distributed throughout the institutional structures of the host society still retaining their ethnic background. This was the beginning of the urge on the governments' part towards structural assimilation.[1]

"In the jungle, lions are with lions, and tigers with tigers, and red birds stay with red birds, and blue birds with blue birds. That's human nature too, to be with your own kind. I don't want to go where I'm not wanted."—Cassius Clay.

The isolation of ethnic groups in Montreal's society is easily shown by classifying some of their private clubs.

Table 39: Parallel Clubs

	Jewish	English	French
Social	Montifiore	Mt.Royal St.James	St. Denis
Sailing	Lord Reading	Royal St.Laurence	
Golf	Elm Ridge Hillsdale Cedarbrook Green Valley Pinegrove	Mt.Bruno Royal Montreal Kanawaki Beaconsfield	Laval-sur-le-lac Richelieu

Strengthening the connections between ethnic groups in Montreal, so that they can all work together with a common agenda, is a daunting task. Somehow a united front must succeed in creating a situation that will allow all these communities to exist harmoniously with the French majority.

Table 40: First Official Language Spoken 3,091,115—1991

Greater Montreal	
French	2,253,405
English	654,800
Eng. and Fr.	130,515
Neither	52,395

Statistics Canada

Table 41: Single responses—Language in Montreal Selected Areas (Map 5)

	French	English	Other
West Island			
Ste-Anne-de-Bellevue	1950	1675	275
Senneville	305	515	100
St-Geneviève	2155	745	205
Pierrefonds	19075	18400	8415
D.D.O.	9920	23285	11030
Roxboro	2410	2300	890
Baie D'Urfé	740	2345	640
Beaconsfield	4150	12150	2620
Pointe-Claire	6410	16825	3365
Dorval	5800	8740	1935
Kirkland	4690	8620	3415
Industrial			
Lachine	21995	8850	3015
Lasalle	34895	21485	13125
Verdun	40970	13925	4055
St. Pierre	3635	830	310
Residential			
Montreal West	455	3655	880
Côte St. Luc	2970	16000	8060
Hampstead	1055	5620	1600
Westmount	3670	12800	2920
Mont-Royal	7070	6260	4020
Grand Total			
Montreal Island	967,435	333,470	369,950

Statistics Canada

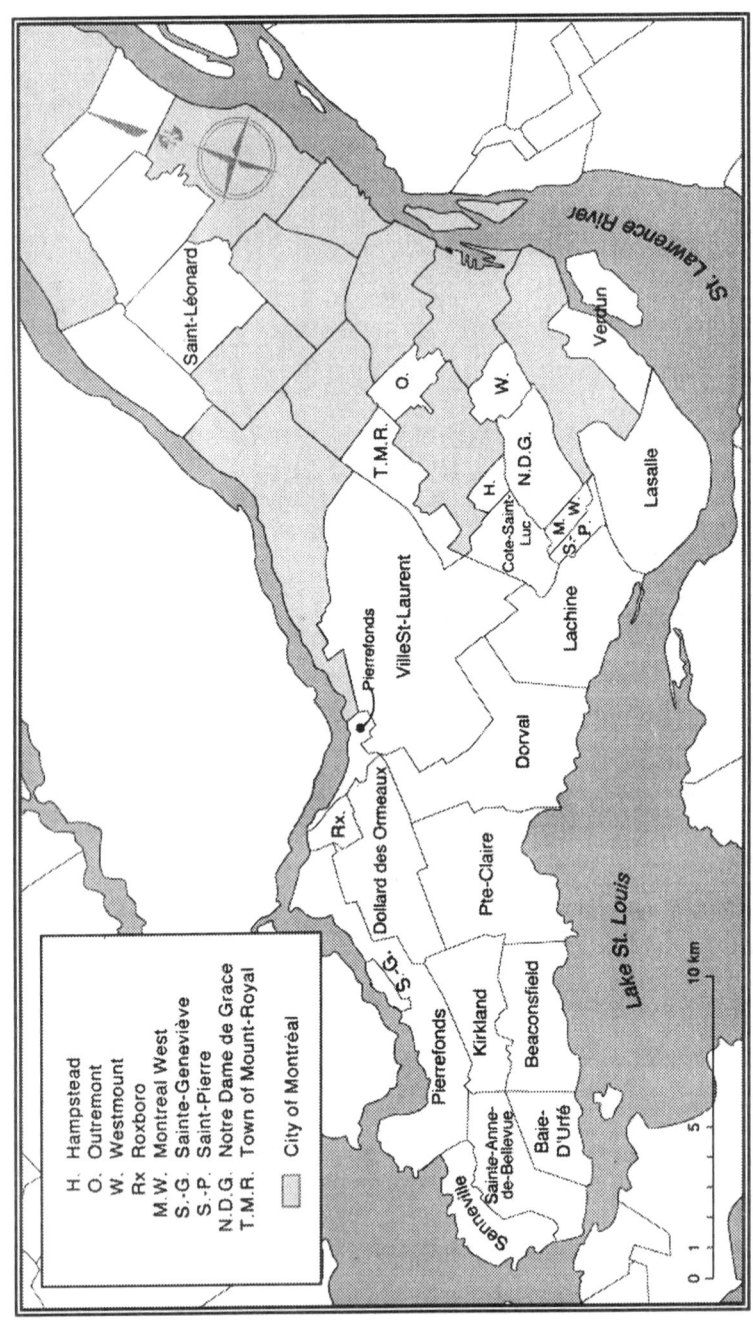

Map 5: Language in Montreal selected areas.

I was amazed at the numbers when I looked at the main ethnic groups. We really have a cosmopolitan city.

Table 42: Selected main ethnic groups in Montreal 1991—Also by language. Greater Montreal 3,091,115

	Ethnic	Language spoken at home
French	1,824,305	2,080,980
British	166,815	440,870 English
Italian	165,735	129,615
Jewish	76,780	- Yiddish 11,255
		Hebrew 3515
Greek	48,575	45,150
African	38,650	- mixed
Chinese	34,355	29,020
Portuguese	32,350	29,780
Lebanese	28,490	- mixed
Latin Am.	24,905	- with Spanish
Haitian	20,145	24,505 Creoles
Polish	20,025	17,075
German	18,935	14,770
Spanish	18,540	46,570
Vietnamese	17,790	15,900
East Indian	16,765	- 6 languages
Armenian	13,675	13,825
Ukrainian	9,940	5,920
Philippino	9,735	5,370
Cambodian	6,700	5,250

Statistics Canada

For many years, Anglo-Canada, i.e. the English, dominated the economies of Quebec too. When the provincial Liberals lost power in 1976, the leaders of the Jewish Community found themselves without any governmental power in Quebec.

"Acutely aware of French Canada's hostility, Jews had nonetheless learned that they could live with it as long as Anglo-Canada controlled the country."[2]

With the current threat of separation from, or association with, Canada confronting Quebecers every day for the last 25 years, these threats have permeated the Jewish Community. Every person other than the French radicals realizes that they must sell the concept of honest democracy and good economics to everyone in Quebec to put to rest all the Referendum rhetoric. Will the Jews help lead the way or will they just move to Toronto? If some of their leaders, such as C. Bronfman leave[3], it could cause a stampede.

The Jewish Community must establish concrete ties with other ethnic communities that include a common agenda focused on the realities of the moment— on schooling, health care, and pensions—to establish a better understanding of each other.

The Canadian Jewish Congress and the FCJA both have committees on external community relations. B'nai Brith and Hillel work on different agendas, and so do the Dialogue St. Urbain and Alliance Quebec. Then there is the Montreal Urban Community Intercultural and Interracial Relations Committee and Quebec's Conseil des Communautes Culturelles et l'Immigration. They are not the powerhouses that they could be unable, as they are, to sway the politicians and bureaucrats in Quebec towards rapprochement.

To confuse the issue, in 1994 the Canada-Israel Committee coordinated a trip to Israel of nine memebers of the Parti Québécois, including separatist MNAs, with representations from the CJC, C-S.Q., B'nai Brith and Can. Zionist Federation. If the Jewish Community in Montreal wants to have dialogue with the P.Q. then they should soften their mentioning of Israel, include the Fed. JCA and other Montreal organizations, and show a commitment to Quebec and especially to Montreal.

It is not just bureaucratic contracts between the P.Q. and the Jewish Community that are needed, but an increase of understanding between the French of Quebec and the Jews of Quebec.

Problems for further External Rapprochement
1. Little contact with other ethnic groups.
2. There is distrust of the entrepreneurial and highly educated Jewish community by the less influential groups.
3. The signals emanating from the different organizations in the Jewish community are mixed.
4. All the ties are relatively new with the dominant political culture.
5. Nothing in common with the dominant political culture.
6. No political clout compared to the influence the community had with the provincial Liberal Party.

Notes
1. Porter, John. *The Vertical Mosaic*. Toronto. 1965. HN 103.5 P6. p.73.
2. L'Anglais, Jacques et al. *Le Québec de demain et les communautés culturelles* Montreal 1990. FC 2950 A1 Q43, p. 252.
3. Lamey, Mart. "Bronfmans sell home" Montreal Gazette, Sept 20, 1997, p.D1.

References
Bissoondath, Neil. *Selling Illusions: The Cult of Multiculturalism in Canada*, Toronto, 1994.
Clay, Cassius (Muhammad Ali) quoted on Feb. 24, 1964. From *N.Y. Times*. Jan. 17, 92: B12.
Jedwab, Jack. 'The Politics of Dialogue: Rapprochement Efforts between Jews and French Canadians 1939-1960, p. 42-74. From *Renewing Our Days*. Robinson/Butovsky.
Kahane, Meir. *Why Be Jewish?* N.Y. 1977. DS 143K26.
L'Anglais, Jacques et al. *Le Québec de demain et les communautés culturelles* Montreal 1990. FC 2950 A1 Q43, p. 252.
Lazar, Barry and Douglas, Tamsin. *The Guide to Ethnic Montreal*. Montreal. 1992
Levine, Marc, V. *The Reconquest of Montreal: Language policy and social change in a bilingual city*. Philadelphia. 1990. P. 119.32 C3L 48.

Also *Gazette* Oct. 26 94: B3.
MacPherson, Don. "Jewish - P.Q. ties" *Gazette* Feb. 17, 94: B3.
Porter, John. *The Vertical Mosaic*. Toronto. 1965. HN 103.5 P6.
Richler, Mordecai. "The French, the English, the Jews, & What's bugging everybody." *Macleans* 77 (27 Aug. 64): 10-11, 39-42.
Canadian Jewish News.
"Rapprochement" May 13, '93: 1-2.
"Minority Relations", Sept. 9 and 16, '93: 1-2.
July 29 1993, p. 17.

CHAPTER 22

INTERNAL RAPPROCHEMENT

Does the Jewish community of 97,000 people, struggling to keep itself vibrant, need any further internal dissension?

Montreal Jews are facing the problems of fertility, outmarriage, youth leaving the community, an aging population, poverty, and dualism, combined with the dilemma of trying to get some cohesiveness between different sects, with their separate customs and philosophical divisions. Something must be done.

Does the Jewish community need a Rabbi supporting the language policies of the Quebec separatists? Or a Jew running under the P.Q. banner? Or the Tash siding with the sovereignists? Or, does it need the increasing isolation of the Hasidim? Or the Lubavitchers proclaim the imminent coming of the Messiah via blatant signboard advertizing, risking ridicule from their own Jewish community and eliciting cries of blasphemy from the religious Christian majority?

Montreal's Jews have a strong traditional perspective.[1] Even the Reform movement leans towards Conservatism and the "middle of the road" Conservatives are quite right-wing. The Sephardim only have few that are not observant. Even the secular ranks in Montreal observe the High Holidays at a higher rate than most other cities in Canada. Added to this is the increase of fundamentalism within the Orthodox community. These changes show an awareness and strength in the community's commitment to Judaism.

The Money Web allows the sincere givers of time and money to do good where they feel it is needed. And for this they receive personal satisfaction, community recognition in the guise of positions in associations and committees, and many other honours. If these people could realize the magnitude of the problems that exist and work to solve them, then much would be accomplished.

Who will lead this internal rapprochement in the Jewish community? First, the Community has to acknowledge that it is possible. Then, it has to see that there is a way to do it in the near future. An unblinking self-assessment of each Jew, who must realize that it is in her or his best interests to become closer to other Jewish sects in Montreal, must be inculcated in everyone in the Community.

Present leaders must lead. New leaders must be found and recognized. Each sect, group, and organization must work together starting at a grassroots level.

Is this togetherness possible?

Problems for further internal Rapprochement
1. Ashkenazi vs. Sephardic
2. English vs. French
3. English/Yiddish/Hebrew/Ladino/Arabic/French
4. Ultra-Orthodox vs. all
5. Female rights
6. Montrealers vs. Zionists
7. CJC, Fed. CJA and other associations in conflict.
8. Cote St-Luc vs. Westmount, etc.
9. Money Web
10. A Strong Leader

Notes

1. Fishel, John "The Quebec Ashkenazi Community" from *Echoes from Quebec Jewry* Montreal 1987 (Monchanin Cross Cultural Center), p.3.

References

Arnold, Janice "Tashel Chassidim on the Side of Sovereignty" *C.J. News*. Feb. 23, 1995, p. 6.

Benaim, Esther. "Francophone Jews and the French Fact" *Viewpoints* Spring 1979,vol. X #1, p. 11-17.

Elbaz-André. "A new immigration to Canada: North African Jews in Montreal." *J. of Can. St.* vol. 13, 1968.

Fishel, John "The Quebec Ashkenazi Community" from *Echoes from Quebec Jewry* Montreal 1987 (Monchanin Cross Cultural Center)

Levy, Elias. "`Ma Communauté à la une' -Une priorité" *C.J.N.* Feb. 17, 94: 2.

Mayer, Egon. "From an External to an Internal Agenda" p. 417-435 in *The Americanization of the Jews*. Seltzer & Cohen (ed.), N.Y. 1995.

Sacks, Jonathan "A challenge to Jewish Secularism." *Spectator* Summer 1990, p. 26-32.

Shiffman, L. Quote from "What Happens if the Rabbi Dies" in *Moment* Apr. 1993.

Srebrnik, Henry. "Torah vs. Trudeau: The Battle for Montreal Jewry" *Eye*, 8, #1, Jan. 1982, p. 1 and 7.

Tzuk, Yogev. *Jewish Communal Leadership in Montreal* Montreal,1984. FC 106 J5 T882.

Waller, H. "Canada" *AJYB* 1992 p. 286.

Weinfeld, Morton. *Quebec Contemporary Jewish Milieu* Montreal 1984 (Inst. Que. de Recherche sur la Culture).

IN - *Montreal* Monthly added section to C.J.N. "Information and insights for young Jewish adults." Started spring 1993. article March 11, 1993, p. 19.

C.J.N.

"Community: future discussed". March 24, 94, p. 20.

"Greater Sephardic role urged" Sept. 27,94, p. 9.

CHAPTER 23

CONTINUITY

I interviewed Peter Schwartz in December 1992. We talked about our meeting at the #1 hearts game in the McGill Union back in the early 50's. The "Immortal" players then were Larry Sirota, Don Paofski, Jerry Shiller, Stanley Cyternbaum, Mel Diner and Sam Diner and Peter Schwartz. I remember the cherry cokes, peanut butter and jelly sandwiches, and the occasional greasy grilled cheese brought up from the cafeteria downstairs.

I only played three times in three years. I lost each game—as a 'fish' always did. The rest of the times, maybe 150, I just kibitzed, being the only "goy" allowed to do so at the #1 Table. Peter and I told many stories back and forth until, in a flash of remembering, I told how Larry S., flushed, with eyes bulging, smote the table with the 'Black Queen' (it's not genealogically correct to use the term then used) and split the 6' x 4' table in half. (I have the idea of having a reunion of old hearts players and having a 45th Anniversary game in the same location—now the second floor of the up-scale McCord Museum—maybe in 1998 —amazingly we are all still in Montreal.)

In an interview with Charles Bronfman, I asked him what gave the Jewish community its first sense of permanence. He answered that the willingness of the leading families—Steinberg, Cummings, Pascal, Reitman and Bronfmans—to lead and unite the community in their fund-raising and communal sense of responsibility gave the Jews of Montreal a feeling of togetherness. This was at a time when the Jewish population was mostly Ashkenazi. The Community was separate from the French and the WASPs, and there was little mixing, or tokenism, prior to the 'Quiet Revolution' of the 1960's.

"Jews tend to thrive in open, pluralistic, moderate, nonnationalistic secular societies".[1] — when given a choice.

Huntington deliberates that as education increases, cultural differences become more important and divisions such as religion, language, and tradition are increasingly more diverse.[2]

"Jews have faced dangers in the past, but this time we may be unprepared to confront the newest threat to our survival as a people, because its principal cause is our own success as individuals. Our long history of victimization has prepared us to defend against those who would destroy us out of hatred; indeed, our history has forged a Jewish identity far too dependant on persecution and victimization by our enemies. But today's most serious threats come not from those who would persecute us, but from those who would, without any malice, kill us with kindness—by assimilating us, marrying us, and merging with us out of respect, admiration, and even love. The continuity of the most influential Jewish community in history is at imminent risk, unless we do something dramatic now to confront the quickly changing dangers."[3]

The strength of the community has helped it through the turbulent years of the 1976 Parti Québécois election, 1980-90s French Québécois Nationalism, and the 1995 Referendum. Today in 1997, the Community must be internally inspired to have a long-term commitment to Montreal.

Torczyner discusses continuity, and breaks it down into two segments: (1) an ability to retain or enlarge the community; (2) to help and strengthen the cohesion of its communal and religious life, as well as its links to Israel and the sense of its own identity.

Examining Cohesiveness

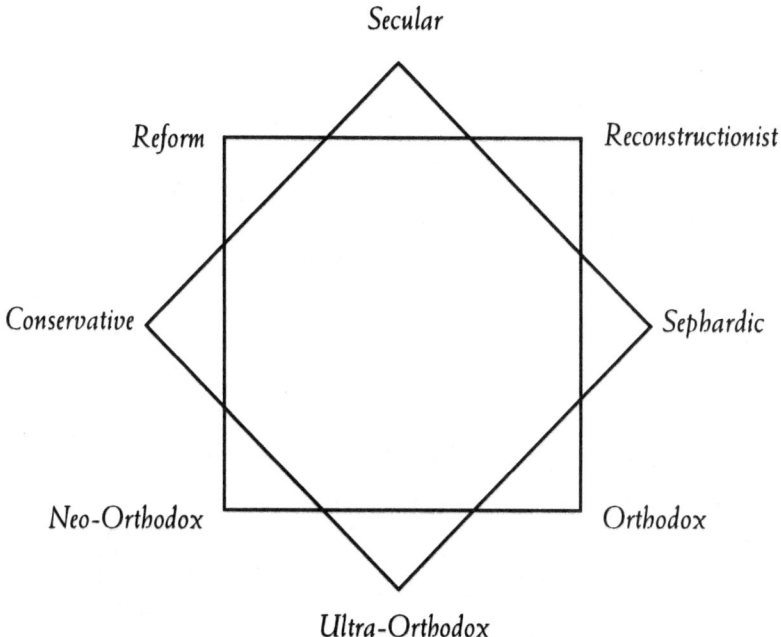

It seems that the 100,000 mark of population is all important to the community. For years, the Statistics Canada census has indicated over 100,000 Jewish Montrealers. Now in the 1990s, the religious and ethnic statistics are below 100,000. The journalists and association personnel have started to use Torcyzner's definition to be able to quote a figure of above 100,000.[4] We have seen that each year a larger proportion of Jewish Montrealers are aged. In Jewish youth, another important group, there is a distressing drop.

Table 43: Jewish Youth 15-24 (by religion)

Year	Population
1971	19,995
1981	14,385
1991	11,705

Statistics Canada

Pro-Montreal Youth Division is a task force of the Fed. CJA dedicated to encouraging young Jewish adults to stay in Montreal. A large colourful newspaper entitled "In Montreal" is published twelve times a year. The Jewish Vocational Service has a contact program that tries to link up recent Jewish university graduates with potential employers. McGill and Concordia's 5000 Jewish students can use the services of the Hillel House and the Chabad House, where direction and support are given to students.

Where does the umbrella organization, Fed. CJA, really stand on this issue of keeping Montrealers, especially the youth, living here ? On the subject of return to Israel? The answer I got was that "the federation supports aliyah but it does not promote it."[5] Added to this, the Canadian Zionist Federation has planted a person in Montreal to promote aliyah. I find that there are many others who are supportive of aliyah and preach it continuously to the Jewish youth. The Canadian Jewish News promotes aliyah even though it is subsidized by the Fed. CJA.[6]

In Montreal, youth retention is the most important factor in the continuity of the Jewish community.

A concerned Jew, Walter Lee, living on the South Shore, created a community there in 1993. In a conversation with him in January 1996, he exuberantly said that there were 154 families identified as having Jewish affiliations. The newly approved organization, South Shore Jewish Community, has received a start-up grant from the Fed CJA. This community (stretching from Boucherville, St-Hubert to Brossard) has a community center, youth classes, and Hebrew classes for adults and children. An amazing on-going story of strengthening a diverse community. Mr. Lee shows it can be done!

A list of vital problems that confront the Jewish Community in Montreal:

Table 44: Problems for Continuity in the Jewish Community in Montreal.

Problem	1996 situation
Immigration	Decreasing
Intermarriage	Increasing
Fertility	Decreasing
Aging	Increasing
Assimilation	Increasing
Loss of youth	Increasing
Education	Decreasing (25% get formal community education)
Woman's place	Needs change to attain commitment
Fundamentalism	Increasing (furthering split)
Synagogue attendance	Decreasing
Secularization	Increasing
Association conflicts	Increasing, as the fight for "Turf"
Available monies	Decreasing, in the future
Jobs	Decreasing
Language problems	Increasing
External perception of Jews	Not changing but soon tribalism will change this to more negativism

In 1997 some heavyweights of contemporary Judaism have written on the problem of Continuity. Dershowitz, Abrams and Gordis have different slants and decidedly different answers to the future possible demise of U.S. of A's Jewish communities.

Canadian Jews, on the whole more traditional, can learn from the U.S. of A.'s problems and results.

Dershowitz again emphasizes a need for visionary Jewish education — usable in everyday life; greater emphasis on success in everyday life versus a life geared to sacred survival; and an acceptance by the Jewish Orthodoxy of secular Jews and intermarriage. All this is to be done to ensure a chance to stop the decline in numbers and in Jewish cultural foundations. Is there any fusion possible? What will assure the survival of Jewish life in Montreal? Cohesiveness plus commitment will promote and will ensure the continuity of the Jewish Community.

Notes
1. Dershowitz, Alan, M. *Chutzpah*. Boston, 1991. p.206.
2. Huntington, Samuel. "Clash of Civilizations." *Foreign Affairs*. Summer 1993, p. 22-49. D410F6. p.24-5.
3. H Bauch :Jewish community in turmoil" Apr 6, 91: B1.
4. Drysdale interview
5. *CJN* - Oct. 1, 92, p. 4 and 5 = very important. Apr. 22, 1993. p.23 & Feb. 3, 1994. p.24.

References
Abella, Irving. "Canadian Jews Have Come A Long Way." *C J News*. June 8, 1995, p. 13.
Abrams, Elliott. *Faith and Fear*. New York, 1997.
Arnold, Janice. "South Shore Jewish Community Growing." *C.J. News*. Oct. 19, 1995, p. 3.
Bain, Jerald. "Declining Ethnic and Cultural Identity: A Challenge for the Jews." *Viewpoints* 21, 2, 1993: 3-4.
Bauer, Yehuda. "Selective Aliyah." *Jerusalem Post*. April 7,1995, p. 6.
Brym, R. "A Symposium: Is there a future for Canadian Jewry?" *Viewpoints* 19, 3, 1991: 1-8.
Bulka, Rabbi Reuven. "Judaism: Integrated or Compartmentalized". *Viewpoints* 10, 3, 1990: 52-57.
Crelinsten, M. "A Symposium the future of Quebec Jews." *Viewpoints* 19, 5, 1991: 1-7.
Dershowitz, Alan, M. *Chutzpah*. Boston, 1991.
_____. *The Vanishing American Jew*. Boston, 1997.
Gordis, Daniel. *Does the World Need the Jews?* New York, 1997.
Goren, Arthur A. *New York Jews and the Quest for Community*. The Kehillah Experiment 1908-22, N.Y. 1970.
Huntington, Samuel. "Clash of Civilizations." *Foreign Affairs*. Summer 1993, p. 22-49. D410F6

Huntington, Samuel. *The Clash of Civilization and the Remaking of the World Order.* New York 1996. D860 H86

Jonas, George. "The End of Jewry?" *Saturday Night.* March 1996, p. 18-26.

Kantrowitz, Jack. "Jews in the New Quebec: Who do we go from here?" *Viewpoints* 10, 1 1979: 5-9.

Kraft, Frances. "The Shaliach of Shlichim." *C J News.* Jan. 95, p. 21.

Lazarus, David. "Community Should Plan for Future Situations." *C.J. News.* June 8,1995, p. 4.

Richler, Mordecai. "A Clear and Present Danger." *Saturday Night.* Feb. 1996, p. 50-55.

Rosenzweig, Uri. "The Organized Jewish Community and the Canadian Jewish Future." *Viewpoints* 19, 6 1991, p. 6, 9.

_____. "The (Continuing) Continuity Debate". *Viewpoints,* #22 #3, Nov. 1994, p. 3.

Schmelz, V.O. "Jewish Survival: The Demographic Factor." *AmJYB* 1981: 61-117.

Schoenfeld, Stuart. "Does North American Jews have a future?" *CJC* 23rd *Plenary Assembly* Supplement Apr. 30, 1992: 46-7.

Torcyzner, Jim L., and Brotman, Shari. "Jewish Continuity in Canada". *Viewpoints* #22 #2 1994.

Torcyzner, Jim. "Continuity." p. 30 from *McGill Consortium.*

Weintraub, William. "The Rise and Fall of English Montreal." (Movie) *National Film Board* 1993. Reported in *McGill Reporter,* by S. Comeau Apr. 28, 1994, p. 6.

Wisse, Ruth. "The Hebrew Imperative". *Commentary* 89, 6 Jun. 1, 1990: 84-39.

Shalom., Toronto Star, Section H, Dec. 2, 1992.

Articles by I. Abella, H. Mietkiewicz, M. Torgor, J. Foster, A. Ages, Rabbi E. Schild, Rabbi B. Tanb, W.G. Plant, Pank Draper, Mira, Friedlander, and Leslie Scrivener.

Westmount Examiner. "Keeping Jewish youth in Quebec.." Oct. 3, 91, p. 12.

Gazette:

H Bauch :Jewish community in turmoil" Apr 6, 91: B1.

"Dropping Jewish by school attendance..." Oct. 18, 91: A4

"To my Jews ready to leave, secrecy shows" Sept. 27, 91: A3.

B.K. Kalbfleisch " Exodus of Montreal Jews Slows, Census Data Show." Aug. 24, 1994, p.1&13.

CJN - Oct. 1, 92, p. 4 and 5 = very important. .

CJN - Apr. 22, 1993, p.23.

CJN - Feb. 3, 1994, p.24.

Viewpoints. "Interview with Irving Abella" (*C.J. News*) May 11, 1995 (#2 '95).

CHAPTER 24

CONCLUSION

A nation dying for thousands of years means a living nation. Our incessant dying means uninterrupted living, rising, standing up, beginning anew. We, the last Jews. Yes, in many respects it seems to us as if we are the last links in a particular chain of tradition and development. But if we are the last— let us be the last as our fathers and forefathers were. Let us prepare the group for the last Jews show will come after us, and for the last Jews show will rise after them, and so on until the end of day.[1]

A vexing quote when thinking of the Jewish community in Montreal. But twenty years ago, just after the Parti Québécois victory in 1976, I. Cotler and R. Wisse wrote:

> Does the uniqueness of the Montreal Jewish community justify a special effort at adaptation to the new situation, in order to protect and nurture the community's many institutions and cultural achievements? Or is the Montreal experience now being revealed as just another piece of evidence corroborating the old Zionist concern that the Diaspora can never provide a wholly comfortable home for Jews?[2]

It seems, in early 1997, that every one in Montreal is on

the defensive. All the hard facts gleaned from books articles and interviews are overshadowed when the factors of Quebec politics are taken into consideration.

This pessimism is not new and the resultant migration has been evident. Some observers contend that the departure of nearly 25,000 Jews from 1970 to 1995 is attributable to some combination of the rise of Quebec nationalism, the implementation of language legislation, on-going political uncertainty, economic instability, and fewer employment opportunities for non-francophones. There is a belief that if Quebec achieves either sovereignty or greater autonomy, the economic and political situation will further deteriorate. What might be referred to as the "comfort level" has continually fluctuated for certain residents of Quebec over the past two decades, but it is true that not everyone in Quebec is affected in the same way by the political situation.[3] In 1995, Shahar's survey showed 66% of Jews were pessimistic about life in Quebec.[4]

In the intervening two years we have seen the machination of the Parti Québécois on the economy and on the life of each person who is trying to get ahead with their lives. When will it end? Parizeau's comment deliniating his plan to declare independence (thereby repudiating all previous signed agreements) has made everyone extra wary of Bouchard, Landry, Parizeau and their cabals.

The Jewish Community, headed by the Fed. CJA, formed a committee in 1996 —the Council on Jewish Identity and Continuity and its goals are:
1. developing educational and outreach programs for Jewish teenagers.
2. developing programs to enhance Jewish educational activities in summer camps.
3. providing increased support and resources to a network of supplemental schools.

4. developing informed educational and outreach programs for families whose children may not be receiving formal Jewish education.
5. supporting initiatives that provide artistic and cultural programs within a Jewish framework.
6. providing support services to international families and their children.
7. strengthening the relationship between synagogues and the Fed.[5]

Great concepts. But when will it happen? The plan is too long term to effect a change soon enough to save the commity from further shrinkage.

Montreal's Saul Hayes put it happily: "The mystique of Jewish survival is the miracle of all time."[6]

"After all the discussing there comes a time to finally act—to act in the defence of the future of Montreal."[7] Where is the togetherness in the community? In the health and athletic fields, the revitalization and expansion at the "Y" is a symbol of continuity and renewal[8] and an attempt to reunite the community. Why not continue this togetherness – a sort of Renaissance – with the community buying a building on Sherbrooke St., near the museum complex of the Montreal Museum of Fine Arts, to have and display the history and present day aspects of the contribution of the Jewish community to Montreal's growth and achievements. This building should house, a Memorial for the 104 Montreal Jews who died to preserve Canada's, Quebec's and Montreal's freedom during WWII, and the Holocaust Memorial Centre (now housed in a subterranean part of the Fed. CJA edifice.).

This would show to Montrealers that the Jewish Community is vibrant and believes in Montreal as a viable place to live.

"A new Jewish Leadership must emerge to supplement the traditional rabbinic and political [and bureaucratic] leadership of the Jewish people."[9]

Who will stand up?

Who will lead?

Notes
1. Cotler I., & Wisse R.R. "Quebec Jews Caught in the Middle." *Commentary* 64 #3 (Sept. 77) p. 55, 56.
2. Rawidowicz, Simon. *Studies in Jewish Thought*. Philadelphia 1974, p.223.
3. Jedwab, Jack."Observations on the Mood in Quebec". *C.J.N.* March 6, 1997, p.9.
4. Shahar, Charles. "A Survey of Jewish Life in Montreal" *Fed. J.C.S. of Montreal*. Dec. 1996
5. F.C.J.A. release " Agenda" 1956
6. Hayes, Saul. "Mystique of Jewish Survival". *Viewpoints* 9 #4, 1976, p. 25.
7. Shapiro, Bernard. Approximate quote from the interview.
8. *Montreal Gazette*, May 2, 1997, p.F14. Announcement of Campaign to Raise $15 Million Towards Expansion & Modernization
9. Dershowitz Alan M. *The Vanishing American Jews*. Boston 1997, p.331.

References
Cotler I., & Wisse R.R. "Quebec Jews Caught in the Middle." *Commentary* 64 #3 (Sept. 77) p. 55, 56.
Crelinstein, Michael and Jedwab, Jack."The Future of Quebec Jews" *Viewpoints*. Vol. XIX #5, 1991, in *C.J.N.* Octt. 10, 1991, p.1.
Dershowitz, Alan M. *The Vanishin American Jews*, Boston 1997.
Hayes, Saul. "Mystique of Jewish Survival". *Viewpoints* 9 #4, 1976, p. 25.
Jedwab, Jack."Observations on the Mood in Quebec". *C.J.N.* March 6, 1997, p.9.

Kaplan, Robert D. "The Coming Anarchy." *Atlantic*, Feb. 1994, p. 44-79.

Kepel, Gilles. *The Revenge of God: The Resurgence of Islam, Christianity and Judaism in the Modern World*. Philadelphia, 1994.

Rawidowicz, Simon. *Studies in Jewish Thought*. Philadelphia 1974, p. 223.

Rome, David (editor) *Canadian Jews in World War II* Part I Decortions (1947 pub.) Part II Casualties (1948 pub.) published by Can. Jew. Congress, in the Jewish Public Library. ML971.0494.C212C.

Shahar, Charles. "A Survey of Jewish Life in Montreal" *Fed. J.C.S. of Montreal*. Dec. 1996

Shapiro, Bernard. Approximate quote from the interview.

Taylor, Charles. *Multiculturalism and the Politics of Recognition*. Princeton, 1993.

Canadian Jewish News, "Future of Quebec & Canada." March 3, 1994, p. 21.

Montreal Gazette, May 2, 1997, p.F14. Announcement of Campaign to Raise $15 Million Towards Expansion & Modernization for the YM-YWHA.

APPENDIX

I.	Food & Religious Days	188
II.	Synagogues & Cemeteries	190
III.	Literature & Film	192
IV.	Lists	195
	- Associated with Montreal	195
	- Canadian Jewish Congress	197
	- Associated with Israel	198
V.	Interviews and Discussions	200
	- Formal Interviews	200
	- Informal discussions	201
VI.	Added Demographics	202
	- World	202
	- U.S.A.	205
VII.	Added Bibliography	205
	- Canada	205
	- Magazines & Journals	206
VIII.	Glossary	207

I. Food and Religious Days

In the Jewish religion, there are restrictions on food consumption. Jews have the Kashrut prescription that delineates dietary practice, allowing organizations to certify Kosher foods and eating establishments. In Montreal, the Vaad Hair, an Ashkenazi organization, has always supervised this until 1992 when the Sephardim Rabinate, whose customs differ, established its own committee to administer the Kashrut. Here again we find different degrees of observance.

There are two food banks that help the great number of Jews below the poverty line. They are the Kosher Food Bank, six years old and downtown, and Le Mercaz, four years old and in northern Snowdon. Both have faced increasing pressure due to the downturn in the economy in the 1990s and the recent arrival of Russians immigrants.

With the dietary laws and the isolated nature of the historic Jewish life, the religious days of mourning and joy were occasions which revolved around a rich cornucopia of food.

Penitence Days
Rosh Hashanah:
The Jewish New Year begins at dusk on Sunday in the fall (on the first day of the first month of the Hebrew calendar). Cooking must start on Thursday as it is prohibited from sunset on Friday to sunset on Saturday. All recipes are very rich due to the gathering of items from the harvest. At this time, Jews implore G-d (God) for a sweet year and a bright future. Note that these are "traditional" descriptions of the meals only. Many Jewish families significantly modify these traditional meals.

Yom Kippur:
A solemn day of reflection and fasting—a holiday, held to remind the Jews of the value of life, held in the synagogue. It is a day to forego worldly pleasure and relive the religious

experiences of life—the Day of Atonement.

Pilgrim Festivals
Passover (Pesah):
This holiday concerns the Jews' redemption from slavery in Egypt. A seven day, relaxing festival observed primarily at home which starts off with a seder meal rich in tradition including unleavened bread—matzoh—and other foods.

Sukkot:
The holiday of Booths commemorating the tabernacles of the children of Israel in the desert. It is just five days after Yom Kippur and by contrast it is held in the home. One builds a Sukkah—a booth, the roof of which must be constructed from something grown in the ground—in which one eats. Throughout the Orthodox areas, one can see the second floor balconies made up into a sukkah. Sukkot reminds the participants of the wanderings of the Jews, and brings one "back to earth" after the solemnity of Yom Kippur.

Days of Celebration
Hanukkah:
The Festival of Lights celebrates the rededication of the second Temple of Jerusalem after the victory over the Syrians.

Each day at sundown a candle is lit in the hanukkiah, an eight-branched candelabra (menorah). The potato Latke (oil-fried) and served with apple sauce, or (not Kosher) sour cream with meat or fowl and a salad are part of the traditional meal. This reminds Jews of the food fed to their Maccabees on the eve of the battle with the Syrians.

Purim:
Celebrates the victory over the Persians. A fun festival where children and often adults dress up and party with sugar pastries.

Fast Days
    Gedaliah
    10 Teuet
    Ta'anit Esthr
    Tamuz
    9 AV

Modern Commemorations
    Holocaust days
    Remembrance Day
    Independence Day
    Jerusalem Day

References

Kashrut: Law & Practice (various writers). *Judaism*, vol. 39, #4, fall 1990: 300-493

Klein, Issac. *A Guide to Jewish Religious Practice* 1979. BM710G79X

Lesser, Julie. "Deciding What's Kosher", Montreal Gazette, Aug. 1997, PF13.

Robinson, Ira. "Toward a History of Kashrut in Montreal: The Fight Over Municipal By-Law 828 (1922-1924)" p. 30-41 in *Renewing Our Days*. Robiner/Butovsky.

"Voice of the Vaad" *Jew Comm. Council of Montreal*, Rabbi IL Hechtman.

II. Synagogues and Cemeteries

The first congregation in Montreal, founded in 1768 under the rituals of Sephardim, was called Shearith Israel. Since then, with many nationalities, sects, and groups arriving in Montreal, there have been numerous buildings housing the various communities. In the CJC National Archives, the Montreal Synagogue Finder (1993) gives an idea of the diversity. In 1994, one found thirty Orthodox, six Conservative, one Reform, one Reconstructionist, and nineteen Sephardic synagogues—all varying in size. Within the Orthodox community, there are synagogues and minyans for the nine Hasidic sects, not counting the Tash in Boisbriand. Each location is near the center of each Hasidic sect, as the synagogue must be within walking distance. There is a Synagogue Council of Greater Montreal a membership of twenty-eight synagogues and all Rabbis can be members of the Board of Jewish Ministers. No control is exercised over any synagogue but pertinent information is passed around. In the most recent *The Montreal Jewish Director*, 1997 listed 36 Orthodox, 6 Conservative, 1 Reform, 1 Reconstructivist and 17 Sephardic Synagogues in Greater Montreal.

In Montreal, one can find numerous former synagogues being used by other religions or groups after the Jewish populations has moved away. For example, at #92 9th Ave. Lachine, 172 Fairmont (Collège Français), a Caodaïque temple at 7161 St. Urbain, 4650-52 Jean-Mance (Garderie Villeneuve) and on St. Urbain (now an Evangelical Baptist Church; the front railing contains menorahs and on the peak of the roof are the 10 Commandments). Also, though all outside markings had been plastered over, Elysée Theatre on Milton contained reminders inside. Unfortunately, it was destroyed in 1995.

The burial societies affiliated with synagogues share parts of five cemeteries. Recently, a number of Sephardic synagogues have bought land on the West Island. One cemetery, the Back River Memorial Gardens, is having hard times because many of the burial societies are defunct. It is completely isolated, surrounded by busy thoroughfares (Jarry & St. Denis) and is far away from any Jewish community.

As suggested, could the Jewish community save and restore Beth Israel of Lachine to become a landmark in conjunction with Parks Canada's Lachine Canal project? Why not turn one of the old beautiful synagogues into the Holocaust museum, if a larger museum on Sherbrooke Street is not established, for example the Bagg St. Synagogue.

References

Arnold, Janice. "Synagogues eligible for provincial grants" *C.J.N.* Feb. 1, 1996, p. 11.

_____. "Rumours swirl around sale of Synagogue" CJN March 7, 1996.

Atherton, W.H. *Montreal 1535.1914.* Vol. #2, p. #1. Montreal, 1914. FC 2947.4 A75

Breckenridge, Joan."Tight Funds Put the Squeeze on Cantors". *Globe and Mail*, Sept.14, 1996. p.A7

Lazarus, David. "Funds needed to maintain old Jewish cemetery". *C.J.N.* Apr. 16, 1992.

Levitt, S. et al. *Treasures of a People: The Synagogues of Canada.* Toronto, 1985, 150 pages. B-L. Folio NA 5240 L49.

Malchelosse, Gerald, "Premiere Synagogue à Montreal." *Bulletin Recherche Histeria* 50 (May 1944) 155-156.

C.J.C. *National Archives*. "Montreal Synagogue Finder." 1st Revised edition, June 14, 1993, Montreal.

III. Literature and Film

A December 1990 issue of the now defunct "Downtowner" introduced me to the delightful writings of Stanley Asher, whose walking trips explored places of Jewish history and interest. Now the occasional article is found in the Canadian Jewish News.

Also, the 350th Anniversary of Montreal Celebration Corporation put out booklets to show off the Heritage Montreal's placement of plaques. These were published by the Gazette in August 1992.

This vital history needs to be gathered together and be put in book form or even CD-Rom.

Over the last five years, the information I have gleaned about the Jewish Community's culture comes from what I've seen and heard listed below.

Museum exhibits
A Coat of Many Colours - McCord Museum
CJN Nov. 19, 92, p. 18, *Gazette*, Nov. 21, 92, P.E. #1.

Tur Malka - 2 centuries of Jewish life in Montreal, 1993

Film
Movie: *Apprenticeship of Duddy Kravitz* - 1974 (120 min.) I.C.C. Leacock # RED A - 014.

Video: *Montreal Jewish Memories* presented by Dan Okouneff, Howard Kay & Stanley Asher. Captured in 2 hours, a wide spectrum of historic Montreal

CBC T.V.: *God's Dominion* segment #2 *By the Word of God* National Film Board. Examines the Lubavitch movement

CBC T.V.: National Film Board *Rise and Fall of English Montreal* (William Weintraub Prod.) Bittersweet description of happenings in Montreal

CBC T.V.: "Whiskey man: Inside the Dynasty of Samuel Bronfman" Documentary on C.B.C. Witness series produced by David Paperny. Feb '96

Movie: *Bonjour! Shalom!* (Gary Beitel Prod.) Documentary - discussing Hassidim vs. French in Outremont. Also on video.

Movie: *Shabbath Shalom* (Michel Brault) Fictional Montreal district St-Paul.

Movie: *Zelig* (Woody Allen)

Theatre

Yiddish - annual festival, see Gazette July 30, '90, Aug. 6, '92 (includes KLEZMER music) produced by Dora Wasserman.

Saidye Bronfman Center:
- a yearly program of events including exhibits in foyer, theatre, and an array of lectures

To Come?

"Towards a Promised Land" *Gazette* May 10,1992, p. F2.

"Between the Solitudes" J. Neidik

References

Ausubel, Nathan (ed.). *A treasury of Jewish Humor.* Garden City. 1951.

Bandy, Nicholas & N. Kattan *Les juifs et la communauté française.* Montreal, 1965. FC 106 J5 J85 (3-12)

Bellow, Saul. *Herzog*, New York, 1964.

Benazon, Michael. "The Pofiles of (Dis)integration: Montreal Jewish Fiction in Engish." p. 149-164 in *Renewing our Days*, Robinson/ ButovlskyA.M.

Brenner, Rachel F. "A. M. Klein & M. Richler" *J. of Can. Studies* 1989 24 (2) 65-77. Fascism in Quebec. Taken from *Am. Hist. & Life.* Ref. McL. 27: p.801.

Caplan, Usher. *Like One that Dreamed: A Portrait of A.M. Klein.* Toronto, 1982.

Cohen, Leonard. *Spice-box of Earth.* PS 8505 D37 S7 1961.

Cohen, Leonard. *Beautiful Losers.* 1966.

Dudek, Louis. *Poetry of Our Time* Montreal,1965. PN 6101 D8.

Klein, A.M. *Second Scroll* Toronto, 1961.

Kattan, Naim. *Farewell, Babylon*, 1976 PS 8571 A88 A 73.

Layton, Irving. *A Wild Peculiar Joy* Montreal,1989 PS 852 A97 W56
    Red Carpet of the Sun. Toronto 1959.
    Waiting for the Messiah

Massey, Irving. *Identity and Community: Reflections on Engish, Yiddish and French Literature in Canada.*

———. "Public Lives in Private: Ida Maze and the Montreal Yiddish Renaissance" in *An Everyday Miracle* p. 129-157.

Nadel, Ira B. "Various Positions: A Life of Leonard Cohen", excerpt in Montreal Gazette. Nov.3, 1996, p.D5-9.

Pearson, Ian."Growing Old Disgracefully - Leonard Cohen." *Saturday Night.* March 1993.

Richler, Mordecai "Inside/outside" *The New Yorker* 67:40-1 & Sept. 23, 91 and all of his books except *Acrobats.*

Robinson, Ira, Anctil, Pierre and Butovsky, Mervin (ed.) *An Everyday Miracle: Yiddish Culture in Montreal.* Montreal, 1990.

Steinberg, Henry. *Backstage at the Palace: An Irreverent Romp through the Hall of Justice.* Don Mills, 1993. Law KEQ 1082 S85

Wisse, Ruth. *If I am not for myself-: The Liberal Betrayal of the Jews* Toronto,1992.

Yelin, Shulamis. *Shulamis: Stories from a Montreal Childhood.* Montreal 1983. Ed. (child) F 1054.5 M89 J59.

IV. Lists

Associated with Montreal

Federaton of Community Jewish Agencies
Communauté Sepharade du Québec
Jewish Community Foundation

Ahavas Chesed
Association of Jewish Day Schools
Auberge Shalom pour femmes
B'nai Brith Hillel Foundation
Baron Hirsch Institution
Bialik High School
Caldwell Home
Camp B'nai Brith
Committee on the Heritage of Jewish Montreal
Communauté Sépharade du Québec
Cummings House
Dialogue St. Urbain
Fed. C.J.A. Council in Jewish Continuity
Funds for Yiddish Culture

Golden Age Association
Heart and Stroke Foundation
Hebrew Foundation School
Hebrew Free Loan Association
Herzl Health Center
Hillcrest Alternative Program
Hillel Jewish Student Center
Jewish Business Network
Jewish Chamber of Commerce
Jewish Colonisation Association of Canada
Jewish Community Council - Va'd Ha'ir
Jewish Cultural Association
Jewish Day Schools
Jewish Education Council
Jewish Family Services of Baron de Hirsch Institute
Jewish General Hospital
Jewish Home Day Care Center
Jewish Hosp. of Hope
Jewish Nursing Home
Jewish Peoples & Peretz Schools
Jewish Public Library
Jewish Rehabilitation Hospital
Jewish Vocational Service
Le Mercaz
Maimonides Hospital
Maison Shalom
Miriam Home
Montreal Holocaust Memorial Centre
Mount Sinai Hospital
Pro Montreal
    ·jobs for graduates
    ·on-going activities to make it interesting to live in
    Montreal
    ·In Magazine - intercommunication
Project Genesis

Saidye Bronfman Center
Shaar Hashomayim's Meals on Wheels
Solomon Schechter Academy
Starlight Foundation
United Talmud Torah of Montreal
Y Country Camp
YM-YWHA
- *Please excuse me if I have missed any.*

**Canadian Jewish Congress
National Constituent Organizations**

Achdut Ha-Avoda
Agudat Israel
Canadian Association for Labour Israel
Canadian Council of Conservative Judaism
Canadian Council for Reform Judaism
Canadian Friends of Peace Now
Canadian Jewish Historical Society
Canadian Sephardic Federation
Canadian Zionist Federation
Emunah Women of Canada
Friends of Pioneering Israel
Hadassah-WIZO of Canada
Jewish Immigrant Aid Services
Jewish National Fund
Jewish War Veterans of Canada
Kadimah
Labor Zionist Movement
Labour Zionist Alliance of Canada
Lubavitch Youth Organization
Mizrachi Organization of Canada
Na'amat Canada
National Council of Jewish Women
North American Jewish Students' Network (Canada)

ORT Montreal
State of Israel Bonds
United Israel Appeal of Canada Inc.
Zionist Organization of Canada

Associated with Israel

14 Yeshivot Hesder of Israel
Agency for Israel
Agudath Israel
American Society for the Protection of Nation in Israel
Asaf Harofe Hospital in Israel
Associates of Ben Gurion U of the Negev
Association of Americans and Canadians in Israel
B'nai Brith
B'nai Brith Women of Canada
Canadian Bar-Ilan BESA Center for Strategic Studies
Canada-Israel Committee
Canadian Association for Labour Israel
Canadian Friends of Amal
     Alliance Israelite de Universelle
     Bar-Ilan U
     Belz Institution of Israel
     Beth Ha-Tefutsoth
     Biotechnical Inst. of Tel Aviv
     Boys Town Jerusalem
     Ezrath Nashim, Herzog Hospital
     Gerer Institution in Israel
     Haifa U.
     Hebrew U.
     Mesivta Torah Terminal
     Tel Aviv U.
     Yeshiva U.
     Yeshivah Aish Hatorah
Canadian Jewish Congress & Agencies

Canadian Institute for Jewish Research
Canadian Magen David Adom for Israel
Canadian Society for the Weizmann Institute of Science
Canadian Technion Society
Canadian Young Judea
Canadian Zionist Federation
Cohen Centre for the Mentally Handicapped in Be'eisheva
Commonwealth Jewish Foundation of Canada
Emunah Women of Canada
Hadassah - WIZO (of Canada)
Herzl Foundation for International Exchange
Ilan Foundation
Institute for Middle East Peace & Development
Israel Aliyah Centre
Israel Bonds, State of (Israel Bonds Jerusalem 3000)
Israel Committee
Israel Cancer Research Fund
Israel Cultural Foundation
Israel Economic Mission
Israel Emergency Fund
Israel Industrial Research & Development Foundation
Jerusalem Foundation of Canada
Jewish Agency for Israel
Jewish Institute of Higher Research
Jewish National Fund of Canada
Labour Zionist Alliance of Quebec
March to Jerusalem (youth projects)
Mizrachi Organization of Canada
Montreal Israel Experience Centre
Na'amat Canada
New Israel Fund of Canada
ORT Montreal
Project Exodus
Simon Wiesenthal Center - International
State of Israel Bonds

United Israel Appeal of Canada
United Zionist Council - Aliyah Department
Volunteers for Israel (Sar El)
YM-YMHA Betsavta-Israel Program
Young Adults for Migdel Ohr

V. Interviews and Discussions

Interviews

Daniel Amar
Pierre Anctil
Rabbi C. Bender
Charles Bronfman
Sam Diner
Steven Drysdale
John Fishel
Michael Goldbloom
Herta Guttman
Klaus Hermann
Peter Jacobs
Jack Jedwab
Norma Joseph
George Kantrowitz
Naim Kattan
Frederick Lowy
Bob Luck
Ephraim Massey
Irving Massey
Lou Miller
Jerry Peters
Carol Polter
Allen Raymond
David Rome

Alan Rose
Nancy Rosenfeld
Peter Schwartz
Jeff Schwartz
Don Seal
Bernard Shapiro
Zavie Sokoloff
Joshua Wolfe

Discussions

Stan Asher
Joanne Berger
Alexis Bernstein
Fred Cantor
Neil Caplan
James Fine
Ronald Finegold
Jack Heitlman
Harvey Jaster
Thomas Kahn
Danny Kingstone
Nicki Lang
Karys Marcus
Adrian Levy
Jeannette Moscovitch
Gerald Naimer
Norman Ness
Saul Panofsky
Norman Rill
Howard Ryshpan
Peter Schreter
Nathan Scott
Charles Shahar
Herb Shapiro

Robert Vogel
Harold Waller
Morton Weinfeld
Len Wisse

VI. Additional Demographics

World Demographics

Table 45: Jewish population in major cities - 1996

Europe	
Amsterdam	15,000
Ankara	100
Antwerp	15,000
Athens	2,800
Barcelona	3,000
Basle	2,577
Belfast	550
Belgrade	1,627
Berlin	10,000
Bordeaux	6,000
Brighton	10,000
Brussels	23,000
Bucharest	11,000
Budapest	80,000
Cologne	1,260
Copenhagen	6,700
Dublin	1,500
Düsseldorf	1,710
Edinburgh	500
Florence	1,290
Frankfurt	5,000
Geneva	4,321
Glasgow	6,700
Grenoble	5,000
Hamburg	1,415
Helsinki	850
Istanbul	22,000

Ismir	1,000
Kazan	10,000
Kharkov	80,000
Kiev	152,000
Lille	3,000
Lisbon	300
Lodz	1,500
London	215,000
Lvov	25,000
Lyons	30,000
Madrid	3,500
Malaga	1,500
Malmo	1,950
Manchester	27,000
Marseilles	70,000
Metz	2,500
Milan	10,000
Minsk	45,000
Moscow	150,000
Munich	4,000
Nancy	2,000
Nice	25,000
Odessa	120,000
Oslo	900
Paris, Greater	350,000
Prague	1,400
Riga	15,000
Rome	15,000
Rotterdam	1,500
St. Petersburg	100,000
Salonika	1,100
Sarajevo	1,090
Sofia	3,200
Stockholm	8,000
Strasbourg	12,000
Sverdlovsk	20,000
The Hague	2,500
Toulouse	25,000
Turin	1,630
Vienna	11,000
Vilnius	13,000
Warsaw	2,000

Wroclaw 1,500
Zagreb 1,028
Zhitomir 20,000
Zurich 6,713
Asia
Bombay 4,254
Damascus 1,000
Shiraz 3,000
Tashkent 50,000
Tehran 18,000
Tokyo 750
South Africa
Cape Town 28,600
Durban 6,400
Johannesburg 63,600
Port Elizabeth 2,700
Pretoria 4,600
Oceania
Adelaide 1,800
Auckland 2,000
Brisbane 1,500
Canberra 500
Hobart 100
Melbourne 50,000
Nouméa (New Caledonia) 100
Perth 4,200
Sydney 35,000
Wellington 1,500
C. & S. America
Buenos Aires 220,000
Caracas 18,000
Mexico City 35,000
Montevideo 28,000
Rio de Janeiro 29,200
Santiago 15,000
Sao Paulo 44,600

JYB 1996

U.S. of A. Demographics

Table 46: Jewish Population centers in U.S.A.

Baltimore	92,000
Boston	228,000
Chicago	261,000
Cleveland	70,000
Detroit	70,000
Englewood & others (NJ)	130,000
Fort Lauderdale	284,000
Hollywood	60,000
Los Angeles	501,000
Miami	240,000
Greater New York	1,790,000
Newark	79,000
Palm Beach	206,000
Philadelphia	250,000
St. Louis	54,000
San Francisco	128,000
Washington, D.C.	160,000

AJYB 1995

VII. Additional Bibliography

1. **Canadian Journals**

    Cahiers Québécois de démographie HB 881 C33
    Canadian Ethnic Studies F 5028A1C3
    Canadian Geographer
    Canadian Studies in Population HB 848 C36
    Demography
    Journal of Canadian Studies
    Journal of Jewish Studies B101 J63
    Revue de Geographie de Montréal
    Others
    Jewish Journal of Sociology DS101 J46 S7

Jewish Spectator AP92 J66
Commentary DS101 C63
American Sephardi BM182A5X

2. **Collections**

Bronfman Collection of Jewish Canadiana
Z6373CM6X
Clés pour l'histoire de Montréal—Bibliographie, Burgess, J. et al. Montreal, 1992 Z1392M65C53
Jewish Communities of the World (4th edition)
Ref. D5 143 J45
Encyclopedia of Jewish Institutions - U.S.A. & Canada
E 184 S5E 53
Selected Bibliography of Research on Canadian Jewry (1900-1980)

Vadnay, Susan (editor) Ottawa 1991 and Cincinnati American Jewish Archives 1995.
World Jewish Directory DS 102. 9W67 - 1991.
Canadian Jewish Historical Society
(5250 Ferrier, #814, Montreal H4P-2N7)

3. **Canadian Jewish Communities**

Csillag, Ron. "Ottawa becoming a 'Hot Spot' for Young Jews." *Can J. News.* Sept. 24, 1992, p. 12.
Gold, Gerald C. "A Tale of 2 Communities: Growth of small Jewish Communities in Northern Ontario and S.W. Louisiana".
Hanson, Lise C. "The Decline of the Jewish Community in Thunder Bay."M.A. Thesis. U. of Manitoba, 1977.
Medjuck, Shena. *Jews of Atlantic Canada.* St. John's 1986. FC J5M42 1986 (3-12)

Rosenberg, Louis. *A Population Study of the Winnipeg Jewish Community*, 1946. F1064.5W7R67

Rosenberg, Louis. "The Demography of the Jewish Community in Canada." *Jew J of Soc.* 1 (1979): 217-233.

Speisman, Stephen. *The Jews of Toronto*. Toronto 1979 (only to 1937) FC 3097.9J5S64.

The Jewish Community of London, Ontario. Toronto 1959 FC106 J5C3

VIII. Glossary

Agunah: Women who have been deserted by their husbands and have been prevented by Jewish Law from remarrying (plural: Agunot).

Aliyah: Immigration to Israel from Diaspora.

Bar/Bat Mitzvah: ritual induction, for 12/13 year olds, into adult Jewish Community.

Bet Din: Rabbinical court.

Chutzpah: audacity, gall

Diaspora: scattering of people of common beliefs and/or backgrounds.

Eretz Yisrael: Land of Israel

Galut-Exile: the condition of the Jewish people in dispersion.

Get: marriage contract controlled by male spouse.

Ghetto: quarter where Jews congregated - voluntarily or forcibly.

Goyim: people who are non-Jews—gentiles.

Halakhah: rabbinical legal decisions that have become Jewish Law.

Hasidim: the members of an orthodox sect; orthodox people.

Hasidism: an orthodox sect.

Kashrut: ritually correct dietary practice.

Kehillah: communal body governing a traditional organized Jewish community.

Kiddush: santification of a blessing over wine at the beginning of many festivals including the Sabbath.

Kosher: ritually permissible food

Mazel Tov: "congratulations!", "Good luck!"

Menorah: candleholder

Mezuzah: a container holding selected passages from the Torah affixed to a doorpost outside a home or office.

Mikveh: a common bath for ritual immersion

Minyan: a prayer meeting, a quorum of 10 male adults needed.

Pale of Settlement: Area in Russia where Jews were confined (1772-1917).

Pogrom: unprovoked attack upon a Jewish Community.

Shabbat: the Sabbath—from sundown Friday to sundown Saturday.

Shiksa: a non-Jewish woman.

Shiva: 7 days of mourning after a Jewish funeral.

Shofar: Ram's horn sounded in the synagogue on Rosh Hashanah and Yom Kippur.

Shtiebl: small informal synagogue

Shul: a synagogue (Yiddish)

Sukkot: seven day festival, building of booths.

Tsuris: Problems, Troubles

Tzedakah: charity

Yeshiva: academy for rabbinic studies.

Zaddik: a pious person

Zion: the Holy Land

INDEX

A

Alexander/Goldfarb families 126
Arcand, Adrien 138

B

Baal Shem Tov 56
Balfour, Lord Arthur James 57
Bender, Rabbi Charles 51
Beramoff 34
Beth Israel 35
Bilu Association 57
Birobidjan 45
Bloc Québécois 156
B'nai Brith 122
Boisbriand 24
Bronfman, Charles 29, 166, 173
Bronfman, Edgar 29
Bronfmans 173

C

Canada-Israel Committee 122
Canadian Jewish Congress 121, 123
Canadian Zionist Federation 123
Caplan, Neil 74
Centraide 128
Chmielniki 69
Copoloff 34
Cote-St-Luc 35
Cummings 173
Cummings, Steven 157
Cyternbaum, Stanley 173

D

Dershowitz, Alan 74
Diner, Mel 173
Diner, Sam 173
Drysdale, Steven 37

F

Federation C.J.A. 121
Ferkoff 34

G

Gameroff 35
Gold, Harriet and Abe 126
Gold, Ms. Nora 99
Guttman, Dr. Hetta 29

H

Hatam Sofar 70
Hebrew Free Loan Association 121, 131
Hebrew Philanthropic Society 121
Hershorn, Ms. Goldie 123
Hirsch 16

I

Israel 48
Issy 29

J

Jedwab, Jack 130
Jewish Immigration Aid Services 121
Joseph, Norma 97

K

Kahanne, Jackie 23
Kattan, Naim 85
Kaufman 34
Kerensky 81
Kielce 137

L

Lambert, Josh 153
Lavery, K.C. Salluste 138
Lazar 34
Lee, Walter 176
Liberal Party 156

M

Marranos 65
Ménard, Joseph 138
Miller, Jerry 29
Miller, Jimmy 29
Miller, Lou 34
Mitnagdim 70

O

Outremont 31

P

Pale of Settlement 46, 56, 69
Palestine 81
Paofski, Don 173
Parti Québécois 155
Pascal 173
Peters, Jerry 23
Poland 47
Polichuk 35
Project Renewal 128

Q

Quebec City 23

R

Raider, Nat 23
Reitman 173
Rhodes 66
Rome, D. 129
Rosen, Ms. Janice 129
Rosenberg, Louis 15
Rubin, Lenny 23
Ryshpan, Howie 29

S

Sainte-Sophie 24
Salonika 48
Schecter 35
Schreter, Peter 30
Schwartz, Peter 173
Sepharad 65
Shearith Israel 85
Sherbrooke 24
Shiller, Jerry 173
Singer 35
Sirota, Larry 173
Snowdon 35
St-Laurent Blvd 34
St-Leonard 34
St. Gabriel de Brandon 30
St. Georges' School 29
St. Jean 24
Ste-Agathe 23
Steinberg 173
Strawczynski, Oskar 143
Swalski 35

T

Taffert, Morty 29
Torczyner, Jim 15
Toronto 16
Trois-Rivières 23, 24

U

Uganda 80
United Empire Loyalists 151

V

Vancouver 16
Victoria 16
Vilnus 45

W

Wappela 16
Wolfpack 125

Y

Yelle, Claude 15